W9-CBT-468

Norwegian
Cooking

for Everyone

"Norwegian Cooking for Everyone"

is a miniature edition of the magnificent book "Norwegian Cooking"

Norwegian edition: «Mat på norsk for folk flest»
English translation: Melody Favish

Publisher:
Kom forlag as
Postboks 865
6501 Kristiansund

Project leader: Svein Gran

post@komforlag.no
www.komforlag.no

Photographer: Espen Grønli

The food photographed by Espen Grønli was prepared and styled for photography by Odd Ivar Solvold

Recipe editors:
Ingebjørg Moe, Export Office for Fish
Heidi Birkrem, Information Office for Meat
Liv Leira, Information Office for Eggs and White Meat
Anna-Karin Lindstad, TINE (Norwegian Dairies)
Britt Kåsin, Information Office for Fruit and Vegetables

Other photographers: See page 160

Graphic design: Unniform AS, Kristiansund
Printer: TiTrykk, Skien

© Kom forlag as, 2004

Norwegian edition: ISBN 82 92496 009
English edition: ISBN 82 92496 041

Editor: Bjarne Håkon Hanssen

Norwegian Cooking

for Everyone

Editor
Bjarne Håkon Hanssen

Senior photographer
Espen Grønli

Kom forlag

Preface

I really like food. I always have. But especially when I was minister of agriculture, I came into contact almost daily with different aspects of the Norwegian kitchen. And everywhere I went, people knew that I like food, and I got to talk about it and taste all kinds of food from all over Norway.

That has inspired me, both in my own kitchen, and to spread the word about Norwegian food and Norwegian traditions. I am especially interested in everyday food. I want good Norwegian ingredients to be part of the meals we eat every day.

I have really enjoyed working with a very well-informed panel of recipe editors on this book. They have helped to make it what I had hoped it would be: a well-written, inspiring book about the food we eat in Norway in 2003. The recipes are based on our own traditions, with some impulses from abroad. A living culture is not static – it develops through impulses from outside.

The Norwegian farmer is proud of the agricultural products produced here. Norwegian agriculture has been spared any huge food scandals. That's because of the ethics of our farmers. Norwegian agriculture gives us good, safe food.

And Mother Nature has given us a fantastic coastline that provides the basis for fishing and aquaculture. Natural conditions and experienced fishermen and fish farmers have turned the ocean into our largest pantry.

Norwegian cuisine rests on a solid tradition, based on good, pure ingredients, in which the flavor of the ingredients dominates the finished dish. That's one reason why Norwegian food has also managed to win favor internationally. It's so gratifying to see how Norwegian chefs win so many international competitions.

"Norwegian Cooking" has emphasized everyday food, though holiday food and weekend food are also included. The book encourages more extensive development of local produce with more focus on regional cuisine.

"Norwegian Cooking" features healthy food. The fresh ingredients that are the basis for many recipes - whether meat, chicken or fish, are all low in fat. Treated right and served with vegetables, potatoes, rice or pasta, they are the healthiest foods you can eat, along with fruit, bread and other whole grains and a number of dairy products.

"Norwegian Cooking" is a book you can use – and I hope it will help you to develop Norwegian cuisine in your own kitchen. Preparing food is a labor of love, both for yourself and for those who are fortunate enough to dine at your table.

Bon Appétit!

Bjarne H. Hanssen

Contents

Small dishes

Anne's best sandwich

1 serving

Guacamole

$\frac{1}{2}$ avocado

4 tablespoons ($\frac{1}{4}$ cup) sour cream

1 garlic clove, minced

2 teaspoons lemon juice

2 slices bread

butter

1 tomato, sliced

50 g (2 oz) chicken or turkey, sliced

50 g (2 slices) Swiss cheese

Mash the avocado with the remaining ingredients. It can be a little lumpy. Fry the bread in butter. Spread one slice with guacamole. Top with remaining ingredients and the remaining bread. Fry until the cheese is melted. Serve with more tomatoes, chopped scallions, fresh herbs and the remaining guacamole.

Bagel *with cream cheese and turkey*

1 bagel or roll

1 celery stalk

salad greens

3 tablespoons cream cheese

4 slices smoked turkey

Halve the bagel. Wash and slice the celery, shred the greens. Spread cream cheese on both bagel halves. Top with celery, greens and turkey. A great portable lunch.

Bagel with cream cheese and turkey

Anne's best sandwich

Tortilla rolls *with cream cheese*

This is a good lunch with an orange and some raisins

2 tortillas (25 cm /10") in diameter
4 tablespoons (¼ cup) cream cheese or fresh chevre
1 red bell pepper

Spread the tortilla with cheese. Clean and chop the pepper and sprinkle the bits over the cheese. Cut into quarters and roll up. Pack each roll separately in plastic. For an easier, less sticky lunch, peel the orange before packing.

Mackerel turnovers

4 sheets (US: 1 package) frozen puff pastry
400 g (14 oz) smoked mackerel
2 hard-cooked eggs
1 dl (⅓ cup) sour cream
beaten egg

Preheat the oven to 225°C (425°F). Partially defrost puff pastry and roll out. Cut out 15 cm (6") circles. Clean the fish and separate into chunks. Chop the eggs. Combine fish, eggs and sour cream. Spoon filling onto the pastry. Fold pastry over filling and press the edges together with a fork. Brush with beaten egg and bake for 15-20 minutes.

Helpful hint
These pastries can also be made with poached or fried mackerel and onion, bell peppers, zucchini, olives, dill and tarragon.

Tortilla rolls with cream cheese

Mackerel turnovers

Shrimp and salad *in pita*
4 servings

2 tablespoons mayonnaise
pinch five-spice blend
½ teaspoon Dijon mustard
shredded salad greens
2 scallions, thinly sliced
1 carrot, shredded
100 g (4 oz) fresh bean sprouts
1 tablespoon chopped fresh coriander
juice of ½ lemon
salt and pepper
4 pita pockets
500 g shrimp, shelled

Combine mayonnaise, five-spice blend and mustard. Combine vegetables. Season with lemon juice, salt and pepper. Spread a thin layer of mayonnaise in each pita pocket. Fill with salad mix and shrimp. Serve immediately.

Basic omelet

2 eggs
2 tablespoons water
salt
butter

Beat the eggs with water and salt. Heat butter in a small skillet until bubbly. Add the eggs. Push cooked egg toward the center, to let raw egg run out. Place filling on half the egg. Fold the other half of the omelet over the filling. Turn out onto a plate so that the underside ends up on top.

Note!
This goes quickly! The egg shouldn't burn.

Ideas for fillings
Grated cheese, buttered leeks or spring onions, smoked fish, smoked turkey, bacon, herbs

Dessert omelet

2 eggs
2 tablespoons any kind of cream
sugar
unsalted butter

Make according to previous recipe. Serve with fresh or frozen berries.

Dessert omelet

Cheese omelet *in bread*

A French cheese omelet is a lovely lunch dish, especially when served with a slice or two of salami on country bread.

2 servings

6 eggs
6 tablespoons milk
100 g (1 cup) grated cheese such as Jarlsberg
salt and freshly ground pepper
butter
2 spring onions, chopped

Beat eggs and milk with half the cheese, a little salt and pepper. Heat some butter in a small pan, add the eggs and cook over low heat. When golden and set, sprinkle with spring onion and the remaining cheese.

Helpful hint
This omelet can be made in advance, cut into 4 wedges and packed in plastic.

Butter 8 slices of bread and pack in parchment paper. When it's time for lunch, place an omelet wedge between 2 slices of bread, adding a little lettuce and tomato, if desired.

Cheese omelet sandwich

Farmer omelet
4 servings

6-8 boiled potatoes
1 onion
1 leek
oil
3 smoked turkey sausages
8 eggs
1 teaspoon salt
$^1/_2$ teaspoon pepper
few slices salami, shredded

Preheat the oven to 200°C (400°F). Dice the potatoes and spread them over the bottom a greased ovenproof dish. Cut the onion into thin wedges. Wash and slice the leek. Sauté both in oil until soft, then place on the potatoes. Dice the sausages and brown without adding fat. Sprinkle over the potatoes. Beat the eggs, salt and pepper together and pour over the potatoes. Sprinkle with salami. Bake for around 20 minutes, until set. Serve with crusty bread.

Onion quiche
4-6 servings

Pie shell
125 g (4 $^1/_2$ oz) butter
200 g (1 $^1/_3$ cups) flour
2 tablespoons water

Filling
2-3 onions
butter
5 eggs
2 dl ($^3/_4$ cup) milk
1 dl ($^1/_2$ cup) light cream
$^1/_2$ teaspoon salt
$^1/_4$ teaspoon pepper
100 g (1 cup) grated Jarlsberg cheese mixed with Parmesan
50 g (2 oz) spicy turkey sausage, chopped

Crumble butter and flour, add cold water and mix lightly together or pulse together in a food processor. Gather into a ball, wrap in plastic and refrigerate for around 30 minutes. Preheat the oven to 200°C (400°F). Press the dough over the bottom and up the sides of a pie pan and prick with a fork. Bake for around 10 minutes, until it starts to turn golden.

Lower the temperature to 180°C (350°F). Slice the onion. Sauté in butter until barely tender. Arrange over the pie shell. Beat eggs, milk, cream, salt and pepper together and pour over the onion. Sprinkle with grated cheese and sausage. Bake for 25 minutes more, until set. Let rest for around 5 minutes before slicing. Serve warm with a green salad.

Farmer omelet

Onion quiche

Invite your friends for cheese

A cheese table is a good alternative to a cold buffet. You can serve either cold platters or a mix of cold and hot dishes. The cheese platters should feature several families of cheeses – some mild, some sharp, some spicy, some firm and some soft varieties. The larger the table, the more variety. A cheese table can be a journey in flavors.

Don't cut up too much cheese. Place a couple of knives on each platter and let your guests take as much as they want.

Count on 250 g (8 oz) cheese per person for a meal.

Purchase the cheese right before serving, and store each cheese separately in its packaging in the refrigerator or other cold place. Do not allow the cheese to come into contact with raw vegetables or other strong-flavored foodstuffs. For the most flavor, cheese should be served at room temperature. Take it out of the refrigerator at least one hour before serving.

Add lots of exciting accompaniments. Cheese tastes wonderful with sweet fruit and berries. Nuts of all kinds are also good. Today you can buy many different dried fruits – these are delicious with cheese, especially if you have marinated them in a little port wine or aquavit first.

Whether you serve red or white wine with cheese is a matter of taste. White wine often goes extra well with cheese – serve both dry and sweet wines, so the guests can make their own combinations of wine and cheese.

Fruit juices and tea are also good with cheese.

Good advice
– Do not purchase too large chunks of cheese at once, even though it keeps well.
– Pack each chunk of cheese tightly in plastic wrap before storing, and change it frequently. Do not store cheese in a humid place.
– Store cheese in a clean refrigerator. It keeps better that way.
– Cheese tastes best when close to the "use by" date.
– The flavor and aroma of cheese are best at room temperature. Cheese for lunch-time sandwiches is good right from the refrigerator, but for extra special flavor sensations, take the cheese out of the refrigerator at least 30 minutes before serving.
– Freezing affects the texture of cheese, though the flavor is still good. It's a good idea to grate hard cheeses before freezing. Use the frozen

grated cheese for cooking. Do not store cheese in the freezer for longer than 3 months.

- *Gamalost* (old cheese) is an exception to that rule and becomes creamier after freezing. Buy a whole *gamalost* and freeze it in chunks when the flavor is just the way you like it. Pack each piece separately in plastic or foil and you have good *gamalost* available whenever you want it. It can be defrosted and refrozen two or three times without deteriorating. This means that you can freeze a whole cheese for a party. Afterward, you can just put the rest back in the freezer.
- Mold cheeses can also be frozen, but they should be defrosted in the refrigerator and used as soon as possible.
- Cream cheeses do not freeze well. They become granular.

- When cooking with cheese, do not allow it to boil, because it forms threads. That's why it's best to add cheese toward the end of the cooking time.
- Count on 250 g (8 oz) per person for a cheese meal, 150 g (5 oz) as a snack, 50 g (2 oz) for a starter, and 75 g (2 ½ oz) for dessert.
- When making a cheese platter, choose a variety of cheeses from mild to slightly sharp to very sharp.
- Do not serve too many different kinds of cheeses together at once. It's better to serve a generous amount of just a few varieties.

Good morning porridge.
4 servings

10 dried apricots
1 liter (4 cups) water
3 dl (1 ¼ cups) rolled oats
1 dl (½ cup) wheat bran
1 dl (⅓ cup) sunflower seeds
3 tablespoons hazelnuts
½ teaspoon salt

Cut the apricots into small pieces with a scissors and let simmer in the water for 10 minutes. Add all ingredients except salt and cook for 5 minutes. Season with salt. Serve with sweet or cultured milk or yogurt.

Oatmeal *with honey and fruit*
4 servings

3 dl (1 ¼ cups) rolled oats
1 dl (½ cup) bran
1 liter (4 cups) milk
1 dl (⅓ cup) honey
1 dl (½ cup) chopped hazelnuts
1 dl (⅓ cup) sunflower seeds
1 teaspoon salt
1 apple

Combine oats, bran and milk in a saucepan. Heat to boiling and let simmer for 5 minutes. Add honey, nuts and seeds. Season with salt. Cut the apple into chunks and add to the porridge. Serve with cold milk or juice.

Sunflower seed porridge
4 servings

1 liter (4 cups) water
2 ½ dl (1 cup) rolled oats
2 tablespoons sunflower seeds
1 teaspoon salt
1 dl (⅓ cup) sour cream
1 dl (½ cup) cultured buttermilk

Heat water to boiling, sprinkle with oats and sunflower seeds. Lower heat and let simmer until the oats are cooked. Season with salt. Heat the sour cream and buttermilk, but do not allow to boil or the mixture will curdle. Pour over the porridge and serve with sugar.

Rye porridge
4 servings

2 ½ dl (1 cup) coarse whole-rye flour
5 dl (2 cups) cultured buttermilk
5 dl (2 cups) full-fat milk
1 teaspoon salt

Whisk flour and buttermilk together in a saucepan. Heat carefully to boiling. Gradually whisk in the milk. Let simmer for around 10 minutes. Add salt. Serve with applesauce and buttermilk or regular milk.

Sour cream porridge
6-8 servings

1 liter (4 cups) natural sour cream (do not use light sour cream or any sour cream with stabilizers, starches or gelatin added)
3 ½ dl (1 ½ cups) flour
1 liter (4 cups) milk
2 teaspoons salt

Heat sour cream to boiling, cover and let simmer for 2 minutes. Stir in half the flour. Stir vigorously until the butterfat begins to leach out. Skim off the butter and stir in the remaining flour. Add the milk and stir until smooth. No lumps should remain. Let simmer for 3 minutes. Season with salt. Serve with your choice of the following: grated brown cheese, lightly sweetened strawberries, raisins, chopped nuts, sugar and cinnamon. For a bigger meal, serve a platter of cured meats alongside the porridge.

Helpful hint
This porridge also can be prepared with equal parts regular and cultured milk. That gives it a fresh, slightly sour flavor.

Sour cream porridge

French toast

Waffles
Around 10

100 g (3 ½ oz) butter
4 eggs
4-5 tablespoons sugar
½ teaspoon cardamom
5 dl (2 cups) flour
½ teaspoon baking powder
5 dl (2 cups) milk

Melt the butter. Combine in a bowl with the remaining ingredients and beat until smooth. Let the batter rest for around 15 minutes. It should be the texture of a thick sauce. If too stiff, add a little cold water. Bake on a greased hot waffle iron. Freshly baked, lukewarm waffles are delicious with sour cream and jam, and cold waffles are good with butter and brown goat cheese.

French toast
2 servings

2 eggs
2 tablespoons sugar
2 ½ dl (1 cup) milk
½ teaspoon cardamom
¼ teaspoon cinnamon
4 slices white bread
butter

Lightly beat eggs with sugar, milk and spices. Soak the bread in this mixture until thoroughly moistened. Fry in butter in a non-stick pan over medium heat until golden on both sides. Serve piping hot with jam.

Tips
French toast was originally served with red berry sauce, and it's really delicious.

Waffles

Pancakes – *basic recipe*
15-20 pancakes

3 dl (1 ¼ cups) sifted flour
½ teaspoon salt
5 dl (2 cups) milk
4 eggs
butter

Combine flour and salt. Whisk in half the milk. Stir until thick and lump-free. Add the remaining milk and whisk in the eggs. Let the batter rest for around 15 minutes. Fry thin pancakes in butter in a non-stick pan over relatively high heat. Flip when the batter begins to dry on the surface and the bottom is golden. Serve with blueberry jam.

For heartier pancakes, use 1 ½ dl (⅔ cup) whole wheat flour for half the flour.

Crêpes Suzette
10 crêpes

Suzette sauce
2 tablespoons butter
2 egg yolks
1 dl (scant ½ cup) confectioner's sugar
grated zest and juice of 1 orange and ½ lemon
2 tablespoons cognac
2 tablespoons orange liqueur

Melt the butter in a pan. Whisk together egg yolks, sugar and citrus juice. Pour into the pan. Add the pancakes and heat lightly. Pour over the cognac and liqueur and ignite. When the flames have died down on their own, the pancakes are ready to serve. Garnish with orange and lemon peel and serve with ice cream or whipped cream.

Crêpes Suzette

Pizza crust

1 crust

25 g (1 oz) fresh yeast
1 ½ dl (⅔ cup) lukewarm water
½ teaspoon salt
2 tablespoons melted butter or oil
4 ½ dl (1 ¾ cups) flour

Dissolve yeast in water and stir in salt and butter.
Add flour and knead until smooth and elastic.
Cover and let rise in a warm place to double. Roll
into a 30 cm circle. Place on a greased oven tray
and spread with sauce.

Tomato sauce *for pizza*

Enough for one pizza

1 large onion
1 tablespoon oil
5 ripe tomatoes
3 tablespoons tomato paste
2 teaspoons pizza herbs
1 tablespoon sugar
1 teaspoon salt

Peel and chop onion. Fry in oil until soft. Chop
tomatoes and add. Heat to boiling. Add remaining ingredients and let simmer, uncovered, for 10
minutes, or until thick.

Here are some suggestions for filling:

Filling 1
Pizza sauce
Shrimp
Mussels
Sliced artichoke bottoms
Chopped herbs
200 g (2 cups) grated cheese

Filling 2
Pizza sauce
Onion rings
Sliced mushrooms
Sliced zucchini
Sun-dried tomatoes, chopped
Olives
Oregano
200 g (2 cups) grated cheese

Filling 3
Pizza sauce
Pepperoni or salami
Sliced tomato
Sliced bell pepper
Sliced onion
Oregano
200 g (2 cups) grated cheese

Filling 4
Pizza sauce
Thinly sliced eggplant
Sliced zucchini
Chopped onion
Sliced tomato
Sliced red and green bell pepper
Oregano
Salt and pepper
150 g (1 ½ cups) grated cheese

Filling 5
Pizza sauce
Sliced sausage
Chicken or turkey ham
Grilled chicken
Cured turkey sausage
Sliced tomato, pineapple, onion, mushrooms, bell
pepper
Grated cheese

Filling 6

Pizza sauce

400-500 g (1 lb) fried fish, in chunks

1 dl (½ cup) grated cheese

1 teaspoon pizza herbs

3 tablespoons shredded basil leaves

2 tablespoons chopped chives

Helpful hint

Vary with smoked mackerel, lightly salted cod or dried fish and vegetables and fruit according to taste. Let the fish simmer in the pizza sauce until done. Spread over the crust and sprinkle with cheese and herbs. Black or green olives are also good on cod pizza.

mixture. Top with corn, pepper and tomato. Bake in the center of the oven for 10 minutes. Sprinkle with cheese and bake 8 minutes more, until cheese is melted and golden. Cool on a rack. Halve each pizza. These freeze well, but separate each pizza with parchment paper.

Pizza pinwheels
20 pinwheels

50 g (1 ³/₄ oz) fresh yeast
2 tablespoons butter
3 dl (1 ¹/₄ cups) skim milk
1 teaspoon salt
500 g (3 ³/₄ - 4 cups) flour

Filling
1 small can (around 70 g/2 ¹/₂ oz) tomato paste
¹/₂ teaspoon salt
freshly ground pepper
100 g (4 oz) boiled ham, chopped
2 red bell peppers, diced
¹/₂ onion, minced
100 g (1 cup) grated cheese

Preheat the oven to 200°C (400°F). Crumble the yeast in a large bowl. Melt the butter, add the milk and heat to lukewarm. Pour over yeast and stir until dissolved. Add salt and enough flour to form a stiff dough. Knead until smooth and elastic. Roll into a 25x40 cm (14x16) rectangle. Spread with tomato paste and sprinkle with salt and pepper. Sprinkle remaining ingredients over the dough. Roll up, starting at one long side. Cut into 20 slices. Place on an oven sheet lined with baking parchment. Cover with plastic and let rise in a warm place for 20 minutes. Bake for around 20 minutes. Cool on a rack. These freeze well, but separate each roll with parchment paper.

Pizza pinwheels

Mini pizzas
12 pizzas

2 cans tuna in water
1 dl (¹/₂ cup) corn
2 dl (³/₄ cup) thick tomato sauce
1 tablespoon dried oregano
¹/₂ teaspoon salt
pepper
1 yellow paprika
15 cherry tomatoes
12 pita bread (12 cm/5") in diameter
150 g (1 ¹/₂ cups) grated cheese

Preheat the oven to 200°C (400°F). Drain tuna and corn well. Combine tomato sauce, oregano, salt and pepper. Mash tuna with a fork and stir into tomato sauce. Chop the bell pepper, quarter the tomatoes. Arrange the pita on 2 oven sheets lined with baking parchment. Spread with tomato

Mini pizzas

Salade Niçoise
4 servings

4 hard cooked eggs
1 can tuna
1 small iceberg lettuce
4 tomatoes
1 green bell pepper
½ red onion
8 radishes
8 anchovy fillets
8 black olives

Dressing
6 tablespoons olive oil
2 tablespoons red wine vinegar
sea salt and freshly ground pepper

Cut the eggs into wedges. Drain the tuna and separate into chunks. Shred the lettuce. Cut the tomato into wedges, the pepper into cubes, the onion into paper-thin rings, and the radishes into thin slices. Layer all ingredients in a bowl or on a platter. Arrange anchovies and olives on top. Combine dressing and pour over the salad. Serve with bread.

Furuly salad
4 servings

125 g (4 oz) cabbage
125 g (4 oz) carrots
2 apples
50 g (2 oz) prunes
50 g (½ cup) chopped hazelnuts

Salad Nicoise

Turuly salad

Clean and slice the leeks into thin rings. Dice the celeriac and carrots. Melt the butter and add the vegetables. Cook, stirring frequently, over low heat until tender. Season with salt, pepper, vinegar and sugar. Just before serving, stir in minced parsley. Serve with meat or fish dishes, but it also tastes good on its own with fresh bread.

Dressing
juice of ½ lemon
1 tablespoon sugar
minced parsley

Shred the cabbage, grate the carrots and dice the apples. Shred the prunes. Combine all ingredients in a bowl. Combine lemon juice and sugar and pour over the salad. Sprinkle with parsley. Serve on its own or alongside fish or meat.

Warm vegetable salad
4 servings

3 leeks
1 celeriac
3 carrots
2 tablespoons butter
½ teaspoon salt
½ teaspoon freshly ground pepper
1 tablespoon vinegar
½ tablespoon sugar
minced parsley

Warm vegetable salad

25

Waldorf rolls

4 servings

½ iceberg lettuce
1 red apple
2 celery stalks
50 g (2 oz) blue grape
10 walnut halves
10-12 slices boiled ham

Dressing
1 dl (½ cup) sour cream
½ dl (¼ cup) low-fat mayonnaise
fresh lemon juice
salt and freshly ground pepper

2 tomatoes, in wedges

Shred the lettuce. Dice the apple and thinly slice the celery. Halve the grapes and chop the nuts. Combine the dressing. Stir the apple, celery, grapes and walnuts into the dressing. Arrange the salad on the ham and roll up. Arrange shredded lettuce on a platter. Arrange the ham rolls on the lettuce. Garnish with tomato. Serve with bread.

Potato dumplings

4 servings

lightly salted stock or bouillon
6 raw potatoes
2 cold boiled potatoes
2 dl (1 cup) barley flour
½ dl (¼ cup) flour
1 teaspoon salt
½ teaspoon pepper

Heat stock in a large pot to boiling. Peel and grate the raw potatoes. Grate the boiled potatoes and combine with the remaining ingredients, mixing well. Make small balls. Let them simmer in hot stock for 25-30 minutes. Do not allow the stock to boil. These are usually served with salt mutton, Voss sausages, fried bacon and mashed rutabagas. The best potatoes for dumplings are Beate, Laila, Pimpernell and Troll.

These dumplings are usually called *raspeball* in Norwegian, but they have many regional names such as *klubb, krumme, kumpe, kumla, raspeka-ko,* and *potetball.*

Cauliflower

with green cheese sauce and cured ham
4 servings

1 cauliflower
4 slices (not too thin) cured ham

Sauce
2 tablespoons butter
2 tablespoons flour
4 dl (1 2/3 cups) milk
½ teaspoon salt
½ teaspoon white pepper
2 dl (1 cup) grated cheese
2 tablespoons chopped parsley
2 tablespoons chopped chives

Cook the cauliflower in lightly salted water until barely tender. Shred the ham. Melt the butter, stir in the flour and whisk in the milk. Heat to boiling and season with salt and pepper. Stir in cheese and herbs. Arrange the cauliflower on a platter. Pour over the sauce and sprinkle with ham and chopped parsley. Garnish, if desired with lettuce and tomato wedges.

Bacon can be used instead of ham.

Potato dumpling

Cauliflower

Stuffed zucchini au gratin

4 servings

200 g (8 oz) ground beef
2 garlic cloves, minced
1 onion, minced
100 g (4 oz) fresh mushrooms, chopped
1 can chopped tomatoes
1 teaspoon thyme
1 tablespoon fresh oregano (or 1 teaspoon dried)
4 zucchini
100 g (1 cup) shredded cheese

Preheat the oven to 200°C (400°F). Sauté beef, garlic, onion and mushrooms until soft. Add tomatoes and herbs and let simmer until thickened. Halve the zucchini and place in an oven-proof dish. Remove the seeds and chop. Stir into the sauce. Spoon sauce into the zucchini and sprinkle with cheese. Bake for 15-20 minutes. Serve hot with bread.

You can also stuff mushrooms and peppers in the same way. Reduce baking time to 10 minutes.

Bruschetta

An Italian appetizer served before a meal.
It's also good as a snack.

3 servings

6 tomatoes
4 garlic cloves
shredded basil
2 tablespoons olive oil
salt and pepper
6 slices day-old white bread

Peel, seed and chop the tomatoes. Mince the garlic and add with basil and oil. Season with salt and pepper. Toast the bread and halve each slice. Spoon the tomato mix onto the bread and serve immediately, before the bread gets cold and soggy.

Onion soup

Onion soup

4 servings

6 onions
2 garlic cloves
2 tablespoons butter
1 ¾ liter (7 cups) stock or bouillon
2 teaspoons strong mustard
1 bay leaf
salt and pepper

Clean, peel and thinly slice the onion. Mince the garlic. Cook in butter over low heat until soft. Pour over stock and add mustard and bay leaf. Let simmer for around 45 minutes. Season with salt and pepper.

Serve piping hot with bread or top each soup bowl with slices of bread with melted cheese on top.

Cauliflower soup

4 servings

1 cauliflower
1 large carrot
1 leek
2 celery stalks
4 parsley sprigs
1 liter (4 cups) meat stock or bouillon (preferably vegetable)
salt and pepper
3 tablespoons butter
2 ½ tablespoons flour
2 egg yolks
1 ½ dl (⅔ cup) light cream
crisp bacon cubes

Clean the cauliflower and divide into small florets. Clean the vegetables and peel the carrot. Cut all into small chunks and add to a pot with the stock. Heat to boiling and let simmer for around 15 minutes. Season with salt and pepper. Strain, reserving the cauliflower florets. Melt the butter, stir in the flour and whisk in the stock. Add the cauliflower and keep the soup warm. Whisk egg yolks and cream together and add a little soup. Return the mixture to the pot and stir until it thickens. Do not allow to boil after the egg yolks are added or the eggs will scramble. Heat to just below the boiling point. Serve with a sprinkling of crisp bacon cubes.

Cauliflower soup

Minestrone   *Italian winter soup*

This is a pure vegetable soup. If you want a little meat, you can dice 150 g (5 oz) bacon or salt pork and fry it before adding the vegetables to the pot.

3 potatoes
3 carrots
1 zucchini
1 small wedge cabbage,
2 tomatoes
½ red chili
1 garlic clove
4 tablespoons (¼ cup) olive oil
6 dl (2 ½ cups) stock or bouillon
½ can chopped tomatoes
1 cup cooked macaroni
1 can large white beans, drained
fresh rosemary

salt and pepper
sugar

Cube the potatoes. Slice the carrots and zucchini. Shred the cabbage. Peel the tomatoes and cut into wedges. Remove the ribs from the chili and mince. Mince the garlic and sauté in oil until soft. Add the vegetables and stir-fry for 4-5 minutes, stirring often. Add stock and tomatoes and let simmer for 10-15 minutes, until vegetables are tender. Add pasta, beans and rosemary and heat to boiling. Season with salt, pepper and a little sugar. Serve the soup piping hot with a sprinkle with parsley, grated cheese and fresh bread.

Fish and mollusks

Baked whole trout
4-6 servings

1 whole trout, 1-1 ½ kg (2-3 ¼ lb)
salt and pepper
juice of ½ lemon
½ fennel, finely chopped
2 celery stalks, finely chopped
½ red bell pepper
½ leek
2 tablespoons minced parsley
1 tablespoon chopped dill
1 teaspoon minced tarragon leaves

Sauce
Cooking juices from the fish
3 dl (1 ½ cups) whipping cream
2 dl (1 cup) dry white wine
fish stock
lemon juice
2 egg yolks
1 teaspoon minced parsley
1 teaspoon chopped dill

Preheat the oven to 200°C (400°F). Clean the fish well, remove the head and tail. If you want to leave the head on, just remove the gills. Sprinkle inside with salt, pepper and lemon juice and stuff with vegetables and herbs. Place the fish on a greased doubled sheet of aluminum foil. Pack the foil tightly around the fish and place in an oven tray, seam side up. Bake for 30-50 minutes. Thick fish and very cold fish need the longer cooking time. Check after 30 minutes. A basic rule: When

the back fin loosens, the fish is done. Stick a hole in the foil and let the juices run out into the pan. Transfer the package to a platter and keep warm. Strain the cooking juices into a saucepan, add the cream (remove a couple of tablespoons to mix with the egg yolks) and white wine and let boil uncovered for 5 minutes. Season with fish bouillon powder, lemon juice, salt and pepper. Remove from the heat. Stir the egg yolks into the remaining cream and whisk into the sauce. Heat until thickened, whisking constantly, but do not allow to boil. Stir in the herbs. Unwrap the fish. Remove the skin and serve with boiled potatoes, asparagus, lemon wedges and fresh herbs.

Baked whole trout

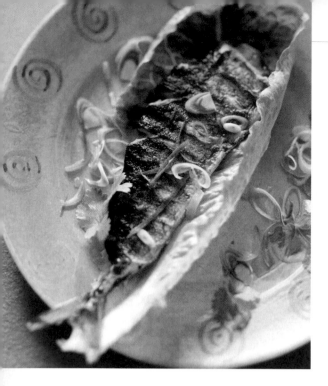

Fried mackerel

4 servings

4 small mackerel, around 200 g (7 oz) each
2-3 tomatoes, sliced
butter
1 tablespoon flour
1 tablespoons breadcrumbs
1 teaspoon salt
1½ teaspoons pepper
2 tablespoons capers

Clean, rinse and dry the fish. Remove the head
and tail and make a couple of slits in the skin on
each side. Fry the tomatoes lightly on each side in
butter. Transfer to a warm platter. Combine flour,
crumbs, salt and pepper. Dip the mackerel in the
flour mixture and fry until golden on both sides.
Arrange the fish on the tomatoes. Add the capers
to the pan and heat lightly. Pour over the fish.
Serve with boiled potatoes.

Fried Arctic char

4 servings

4 Arctic char
salt and pepper
4 tablespoons (¼ cup) minced fresh herbs, such
as basil, parsley and rosemary
2 tablespoons olive oil
2 tablespoons butter

Potato purée

1 kg (2 ¼ lb) potatoes
2 dl (¾ cup) 2% milk
1 dl (½ cup) light cream

Tomato-fennel sauce

4 plum tomatoes, peeled and coarsely chopped
1 fennel, finely chopped
½ shallot, minced
2 tablespoons tomato paste
2 tablespoons olive oil

Remove the gills and season the fish with salt
and pepper. Stuff the fish with vegetables and
herbs. You can use one or more types of herbs,
as desired. Use less if using only rosemary. Heat
the olive oil in a frying pan, then add the butter.
Fry the fish for 3-4 minutes per side. Whole char
is also good grilled. Brush with olive oil or melted
butter and grill in a double rack.

Cook the potatoes, drain and mash. Heat milk,
cream and butter and gradually mix into the
potatoes until light and fluffy. You may not need
to use all the liquid. Season with salt and pepper.

Fried Arctic char

Fried Arctic char can be served with a variety of
side dishes. Boiled potatoes and a mixed salad
with sour cream dressing are a good alternative.
Or make a sour cream sauce by adding 2 dl
(1 cup) sour cream or crème fraiche to the pan
after the fish is cooked. Heat to boiling and serve
alongside the fish with potatoes and marinated
cucumbers.

Fried salmon

Fried salmon

4 servings

800 g (1 ¾ lb) salmon, in slices or fillets
2 tablespoons flour
1 teaspoon salt
½ teaspoon pepper
½ teaspoon dried thyme
butter and/or oil

Wash and dry the fish. Combine flour, salt and
herbs. Coat the fish on both sides with the seaso-
ned flour and fry in butter or a mixture of butter
and oil in a hot pan until golden. Arrange the fish
on a hot platter and serve with boiled potatoes,
sour cream and cucumber salad.

Cucumber salad

1 seedless cucumber
2 dl (¾ cup) water
3 tablespoons clear vinegar
3 tablespoons sugar
2 tablespoons finely diced bell pepper

Slice the cucumber with a cheese plane and place
in a bowl. Combine water, vinegar, sugar and a
little pepper and pour over the cucumber slices.
Refrigerate until serving. Just before serving,
sprinkle with bell pepper.

Norwegian-style cod

4 servings

300 g (10 oz) cod liver
salt
1 teaspoon vinegar
5-6 peppercorns
500 g (1 lb) cod roe
fresh dill (optional)
1 ½ kg (3 lb) fresh cod, in slices

Preparing the liver
Remove any membrane and large veins from the
liver, rinse and dry well. Heat 2 dl (1 cup) water
with 2 teaspoons salt, vinegar and peppercorns
to boiling. Add the liver, lower the heat and let
simmer for 20 minutes. Some of the liver fat
melts into the cooking liquid, and together with
the pepper and vinegar, it makes a good sauce
for the fish.

Preparing cod roe
Heat 5 dl (2 cup) water with 1 ½ teaspoons salt
to boiling. Wash the roe and wrap in parchment
paper or plastic foil to keep whole. Let simmer
for 20 40 minutes. Add fresh dill to the cooking
water for extra flavor. If the roe is to be fried
later, let it cool in the cooking liquid.

Cooking the fish
Heat 1 liter (quart) water with ½ dl (3 ½ tablespoons) salt to boiling. Remove the pot from the
heat and add the fish. Reheat to boiling, set the
pot off to one side and let the fish simmer for
around 4 minutes.

Serve the cod on heated plates with slices of cod
roe, liver and boiled potatoes.

Making a fish "butterfly"

Making a fish "butterfly"

This way of dividing a fish fillet is used primarily for salmon and trout. Start with a boneless fillet with the skin on. Scale and scrub the skin thoroughly. Cut the fillet into 3 cm (1 ¼") thick slices. Cut each in half down to the skin, but do not cut through. Fold out the two sections like a butterfly, so that the skin sides touch underneath.

See illustration.

Salmon butterfly

with mushrooms and nut jus
4 servings

800 g (1 ¾ lb) salmon butterflies
2 tablespoons butter
3 tablespoons olive oil
1 teaspoon salt
½ teaspoon coarsely ground pepper mix

Nut jus
500 g (1 lb) mixed mushrooms, cultivated or wild
4 potatoes, peeled and cubed
1 dl (⅓ cup) walnut oil
2 tablespoons coarsely chopped walnuts

2 dl (¾ cup) fish stock
2 tablespoons butter
salt and pepper
2 teaspoons chopped fresh thyme

Make the nut jus first. Clean the mushrooms and cut into bite-size pieces. Sauté the potatoes and mushrooms in walnut oil. Add the nuts and stock. Simmer until the potatoes are tender. Stir in the butter and season with salt, pepper and thyme. Sauté the salmon in butter and oil until golden on both sides. Season with salt and pepper. Serve with a fresh green salad with lemon or vinaigrette dressing.

Butterflied salmon is also good with mashed potatoes and mustard sauce. Use a sauce for *gravlaks* and serve with coleslaw.

Salmon butterfly with mushrooms and nut jus

Sautéed halibut

4 servings

800 g (1 ¾ lb) halibut, in slices or fillets
1 dl (scant ½ cup) salt
1 liter (quart) water
2 tablespoons butter
3 tablespoons olive oil
1 teaspoon crushed rosé pepper

Hollandaise sauce

3 egg yolks
150 g (5 oz) butter, melted
salt and white pepper
lemon juice

Halibut is extra juicy if soaked in brine before cooking. Clean and rinse the fish. Dissolve the salt in the water and add the fish. Let soak for 10 minutes. Remove and dry thoroughly. Fry in a mixture of butter and olive oil for 2-3 minutes per side. Sprinkle with crushed pepper. For the sauce, beat the egg yolks in a double boiler until frothy. Beat in the butter by the tablespoon. Season with salt, pepper and lemon juice. If the sauce is too thick, add a little fish stock. Serve the fish with boiled potatoes, green beans and hollandaise sauce

For a change of pace, try horseradish cream with fried halibut

Horseradish cream

2 dl (1 cup) whipping cream
2 tablespoons freshly grated horseradish
½ teaspoon sugar
½ teaspoon salt
vinegar

Whip the cream and stir in the horseradish. Season with sugar, salt and a little vinegar.

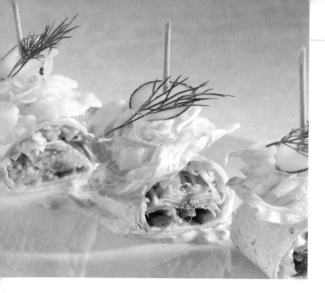

Fried herring

with several accompaniments
4 servings

8 herring fillets, skinless and boneless
1 dl (½ cup) flour
1 teaspoon salt
½ teaspoon pepper
butter

Dressing
1 dl (½ cup) mayonnaise
1 dl (½ cup) yogurt
1 tablespoon capers
1 tablespoon chopped pickle
½ teaspoon minced red chili pepper

Accompaniments
shredded iceberg lettuce
8 tortilla wraps
10 radishes, in sticks
½ cucumber, in sticks
1 red bell pepper, in strips
2 tomatoes, sliced
1 red onion, thinly sliced
parsley

Fried herring in tortilla wrap

Dry the herring well. Dip in a mixture of flour, salt and pepper and fry in butter on both sides until golden. Combine all ingredients for dressing. Place lettuce on a tortilla and top with a herring fillet. Add vegetables and spoon over dressing. Roll up and enjoy!

Alternative
Serve the fried herring with potatoes instead of tortillas. Toss lettuce and vegetables and serve the dressing on the side.

Warm tomato salad for fried herring
6 tomatoes
1 onion
olive oil
2 tablespoons shredded basil
salt and pepper
2 tablespoons minced parsley

Slice tomatoes and onion. Sauté the onion in oil, add basil and season with salt and pepper. Add the tomato slices to the onion mixture and heat. Place tomato slices on the fried herring fillets. Drizzle over a little onion-oil mixture and sprinkle with parsley.

Fried plaice or flounder

with tomato sauce
4 servings

800 g (1 ¾ lb) plaice or flounder fillets
2-3 tablespoons flour
1 teaspoon salt
½ teaspoon freshly ground pepper
2 tablespoons butter
3 tablespoons olive oil

Tomato sauce

1 garlic clove, minced
½ dl (3 ½ tablespoons) olive oil
1 can (14 oz) chopped tomatoes (or 6 fresh, peeled, seeded and chopped)
4 tablespoons (¼ cup) white wine
4 tablespoons (¼ cup) shredded fresh basil
salt and pepper
sugar
8-10 black olives

Dip the fish in a mixture of flour, salt and pepper and fry in butter and olive oil until golden on both sides. Sauté the garlic in oil for a few minutes. Add tomatoes and heat to boiling. Add wine and basil and simmer for a few minutes. Season with salt, pepper and a little sugar, if desired. Serve the fried flounder with cooked pasta and tomato sauce. Garnish with olives.

Try fried flounder with onion compote, steamed spinach and boiled potatoes

Onion compote
4 servings

8-10 shallots
1 garlic clove
3 tablespoons butter
2 tablespoons water
1 tablespoon chopped fresh thyme or
1 teaspoon dried
3 springs fresh rosemary
juice of 1 lime
½ teaspoon salt
½ teaspoon freshly ground pepper

Mince shallots and garlic. Sauté in butter and water until the water has evaporated. Add the herbs and lime juice. Season with salt and pepper.

Fish *in a packet*
4 servings

600-800 g (1 1/3- 1 ¾ lb) boneless, skinless salmon fillet
400 g (14 oz) mixed frozen vegetables
1 teaspoon salt
½ teaspoon pepper
1 sprig fresh thyme or 1 teaspoon dried
juice and grated zest of 1 orange

Preheat the oven to 200°C (400°F). Cut the fish into 4 pieces of equal size. Divide the vegetables among 4 sheets of aluminum foil (50 cm (20″) wide) or arrange in a greased ovenproof dish. Top with the fish. Sprinkle with salt, pepper, thyme, orange zest and juice. Pack foil tightly around each package or cover the ovenproof dish with foil. Bake for 10-15 minutes (the longer time when prepared in the ovenproof dish). Serve in the packets with baked potato wedges.

Alternative
Use fresh vegetables instead of frozen. Try a com-

bination of diced carrot, sliced leek and broccoli florets. Blanch for 1 minute before   placing in packets.

Baked potato wedges

6-8 potatoes
2 tablespoons olive oil
1 teaspoon chopped fresh thyme
salt and pepper

Preheat the oven to 200°C (400°F). Scrub the potatoes well and cut into wedges. Place on a greased baking sheet. Drizzle with oil and sprinkle with thyme, salt and pepper. Bake for around 40 minutes.

Trout *with bell pepper sauce*
4 servings

600-800g (1 ½ lb-1 ¾ lb) boneless, skinless trout fillet
1 teaspoon salt
½ teaspoon white pepper
1 teaspoon crushed rose pepper
2 teaspoons butter

Bell pepper sauce

1 red bell pepper
1 green bell pepper
1 tablespoon olive oil
3 tablespoons shredded fresh basil
½ teaspoon rose pepper
4 dl (1 ⅔ cups) fish stock
1 teaspoons cornstarch
1 dl (½ cup) light cream
salt

Preheat the oven to 175°C (350°F). Cut the fish into serving pieces and placed in a greased oven-proof dish. Sprinkle with salt, and both peppers. Dot with butter. Bake for 10-15 minutes. Make

the sauce while the fish is cooking. Dice the peppers and sauté in oil. Add basil, pepper and stock and reduce over high heat until around ⅓ of the original amount remains. Stir the cornstarch into the cream and whisk into the pepper mixture. Heat to boiling. Adjust the seasoning. Serve the fish with sauce, potatoes and broccoli.

Trout with bellpepper sauce

Fried pollock *with onions*
4 servings

800 g (1 ¹/₃-1 ³/₄ lb) boneless, skinless pollock fillet
1 teaspoon salt
¹/₂ teaspoon pepper
3 tablespoons flour
2 tablespoons butter
1-2 red onions, in slices or wedges
1-2 onions, in slices or wedges
2 garlic cloves, minced
1 dl (¹/₃ cup) chopped chives

Cut the fish into serving pieces and sprinkle with salt and pepper. Dip in flour. Melt the butter and heat until golden. Fry the fish on both sides. Fry onion and garlic in the remaining butter until soft. Sprinkle with salt, pepper and chives. Serve with boiled potatoes, grated carrots and crème fraiche.

Fried pollock is also good with warm tortillas, taco sauce, sour cream and tomato, bell pepper and cucumber slices.

Fish and chips
4 servings

Batter
4 tablespoons (¹/₄ cup) flour
1 teaspoon salt
1 teaspoon oil
1 ¹/₂ dl (²/₃ cup) water
2 egg whites

Tartar sauce
1 ¹/₂ teaspoons English mustard
1 ¹/₂ dl (²/₃ cup) mayonnaise
1 teaspoon minced green olive
¹/₂ teaspoon minced capers
1 teaspoon minced chives
1 teaspoon minced parsley
¹/₂ teaspoon minced sour pickle
oil
4 cod fillets of equal size,
around 175 g (6 oz) each

Whisk together flour, salt, oil and half the water for the batter. Whisk in the remaining water. Let the batter rest for a while. Combine all ingredients in the tartar sauce and refrigerate. Heat the oil until it bubbles around a wooden spoon handle. Dip the fish in the batter, letting any excess batter run off. Fry in the hot oil until golden and crispy. Drain on paper towels and sprinkle with salt. Serve with fried potatoes and tartar sauce.

Fish and chips

Seiwok

Stir-fried pollock

4 servings

800 g (1 ¹/₃-1 ³/₄ lb) boneless, skinless pollock fillet
1 dl (¹/₃ cup) corn oil
1 teaspoon salt
¹/₂ teaspoon freshly ground pepper
1 red onion, in thin wedges
1 carrot, in strips
150 g (5 oz) broccoli, in small florets
1 dl (1/2 cup) bean sprouts
100 g (4 oz) fresh spinach, shredded
2 tablespoons sweet chili sauce
3 tablespoons soy sauce
3 tablespoons fish sauce
a few drops sesame oil
¹/₂ dl (¹/₄ cup) fresh chopped coriander

Cut the fish into 2-3 cm (1") cubes. Heat the oil in a wok and stir fry the fish on all sides. Sprinkle with salt and pepper and remove from the pan. Stir-fry the vegetables in order. Add the sauces, sesame oil and fish and let simmer for 1 minute. Serve over egg noodles and garnish with coriander.

Helpful hint

This dish is also good over rice. Vary the vegetables by using shredded Chinese cabbage instead of spinach.

Fish for a prince
A traditional fish dish

This is a very special dish from Bergen that was composed in honor of a visiting Swedish prince over 100 years ago. The prince wanted cod for dinner, and the recipe was invented to avoid having to make poached cod for so many guests. The dish is not as simple as it sounds.

Fish for a prince is composed of cod fillets that are poached in lightly salted water until barely done. They are then placed on a hot platter, covered with béchamel sauce and garnished with asparagus, lobster and puff pastry triangles.

There are many variations of this dish. The fish is prepared in the same way, but the side dishes are different.

4 servings

800 g (1 ¹⁄₃-1 ³⁄₄ lb) boneless, skinless cod fillet
5 dl (2 cups) water
1 teaspoon salt

Sauce
2 tablespoons butter
2 ¹⁄₂ tablespoons flour
3 dl (1 ¹⁄₄ cups) fish stock
2 dl (1 cup) light cream

2 egg yolks
1 tablespoon lemon juice

Poach the fish, preferably in one layer, in water with salt, until just barely done, around 5 minutes. Arrange the fish overlapping on a heated platter. Melt the butter and stir in the flour. Let cook slightly. Whisk in the stock and cream, and let simmer for around 5 minutes. Remove from the heat, whisk in the egg yolks, and cook until thickened. Season to taste with lemon juice. Pour over the fish. Garnish with shrimp, asparagus spears and chopped parsley. Serve with boiled potatoes and mixed vegetables.

Cod with sweet and sour sauce

Cod *with sweet and sour sauce*
4 servings

600-800 g (1 $^1/_3$-1 $^3/_4$ lb) boneless, skinless cod or haddock fillets
2 teaspoons mustard
3 tablespoons flour
1 teaspoon salt
$^1/_2$ teaspoon pepper
butter and/or oil

Sweet and sour sauce
1 small onion
$^1/_2$ green bell pepper
$^1/_2$ small carrot
1 tablespoon oil
1 teaspoon tomato paste
2 tablespoons ketchup
2 pineapple rings, in chunks
2 tablespoons vinegar
2 tablespoons sugar
1 tablespoon soy sauce
2 dl (1 cup) vegetable stock
2 teaspoons cornstarch
$^1/_2$ dl ($^1/_4$ cup) pineapple juice
shredded parsley

Cut the fish into serving pieces and spread with mustard. Combine flour, salt and pepper. Dip the fish in the mixture and fry in oil until golden on both sides. Chop the onion, cut the pepper into strips and the carrot into slices. Sauté in oil for 3 minutes. Stir in the tomato paste and ketchup. Add pineapple, vinegar, sugar soy sauce and stock and heat to boiling. Stir the cornstarch into the pineapple juice and whisk into the sauce. Simmer, stirring often, until the sauce is shiny and thick. Garnish with parsley. Serve over rice.

Whale *with mushrooms and berries*
4 servings

600 g (1 ⅓ lb) whale meat, partially frozen
butter
8 fresh mushrooms
3 ½ tablespoons water
2 dl (1 cup) crème fraiche
1 teaspoon crushed juniper berries
salt and pepper
2 tablespoons fresh blueberries
2 tablespoons fresh lingonberries
2 tablespoons fresh cloudberries

Cut the meat into thin slices while still partially frozen. Sauté quickly in butter in a hot skillet. Slice the mushrooms and add. Fry for a few minutes. Add the water, crème fraiche and juniper berries and heat to boiling. Season with salt and pepper. Carefully stir in the berries. Serve with mashed potatoes.

Whale *as beef*
4 servings

800 g (1 ¾ lb) whale meat
1 red onion
100 g (4 oz) zucchini
1 yellow bell pepper
butter
salt and pepper

Whale as beef

Cut the meat into 4 pieces of equal size. Slice the onion and zucchini. Cut the pepper into strips. Sauté in butter until soft but not brown. Remove from the pan and keep warm. Sprinkle with salt and pepper. Fry the meat in browned butter for around 3 minutes per side. Season to taste. Arrange the meat on a bed of the vegetable mixture and serve with baked potatoes.

Fish stock *Basic recipe*

Around 2 kg (4 $1/2$ lb) fish trimmings, heads,
backbones or small fish
green part of a leek
$1/2$ onion
chunk celeriac
1 teaspoon peppercorns
1 bay leaf
1 $1/2$ liter (6 cups) water
2 tablespoons salt

Wash the trimmings and fish well. Remove all
blood and gills. Clean and cut the vegetables into
large chunks. Place everything in a pot and add
cold water to just cover. Heat to boiling and let
cook at a rolling boil for 1 minute. Skim well.
Lower the heat and let simmer for 20 minutes.
Skim frequently. When the stock is finished, strain
through a fine sieve or through a clean kitchen
towel. For a stronger flavor or a more concentra-
ted stock that takes up less room in the freezer,
reduce by half.

Classic basic sauces

White wine sauce

4 servings

3 shallots
1 tablespoon butter
2 dl (1 cup) white wine
5 dl (2 cups) fish stock
3 dl (1 $1/4$ cups) whipping cream
salt and pepper

Mince the shallots and sauté in butter until shiny.
Add the wine and stock and reduce by half. Add
cream and reduce until thickened. Strain and season with salt and pepper. If desired, add fresh

herbs right before serving. Use the same herbs as
in the fish dish.

Light fish sauce

4 servings

2 tablespoons butter
3-4 tablespoons flour
4 dl (1 $2/3$ cups) fish stock
1 teaspoon salt
$1/2$ teaspoon white pepper
chopped herbs (optional)

Melt butter and stir in flour. Let cook for a minute or two. Gradually whisk in the stock. Let simmer until thickened. Season with salt and pepper.
Milk or light cream can be used in place of some
of the stock. Add herbs as desired. Remember to
add fresh herbs right at the end, while dried
herbs should be added at the beginning, to develop flavor and aroma. Curry powder and tomato
paste should be sautéed with the onion for best
flavor development.

Bechamel sauce (white sauce)

4 servings

2 tablespoons butter
3 tablespoons flour
4 dl (1 $2/3$ cups) milk
$1/2$ teaspoon salt
$1/2$ teaspoon nutmeg

Melt butter and stir in flour. Let cook for a minute or two. Gradually whisk in the milk. Let
simmer until thickened. Season with salt and nutmeg.

Fish stew

300 g (10 oz) rutabaga
300 g (10 oz) carrots
600 g (1 ⅓ lb) potatoes
2 liters (8 ¼ cups) water
2 teaspoons salt
1 kg (2 ¼ lb) boneless, skinless fish fillet
1 teaspoon sugar
1 teaspoon 7% vinegar
chopped parsley

Clean rutabaga and carrots and cut into 1x3 cm sticks. Peel and rinse potatoes and cut into chunks. Heat water and salt to boiling. Cook potatoes for around 5 minutes, then add the other vegetables and cook until almost tender. Cut the fish into chunks and add. Let simmer for 2-3 minutes. Season with salt, sugar and vinegar. Just before serving, sprinkle with parsley.

Monkfish and halibut are good in this dish, but cod and pollock also work well.

Easy everyday soup

1 packet dehydrated fish soup
1 onion, coarsely chopped
1 carrot, diced
½ leek, thinly sliced
1 dl (½ cup) light cream

100 g (4 oz) fish pudding or fish meatballs
50 g (2 oz) peeled shrimp (optional)

Follow the directions on the soup packet, but use 1 dl (1/2 cup) less liquid. Add the vegetables and cook for the required time. Add cream and heat to boiling. Add the fish pudding and let simmer until heated through. Add shrimp. Readjust the seasoning.

Bouillabaisse means a stock that has been reduced. Bouillabaisse originated in southern France. The dish is called a soup, but it is often so rich and full of ingredients that it can be called a stew. It is based on local ingredients and comes in many different versions. This recipe is adapted to include Norwegian ingredients – shall we call it à la norvegienne?

Bouillabaisse *à la norvegienne*
4-6 servings

200 g (7 oz) boneless, skinless halibut fillet
200 g (7 oz) boneless, skinless wolffish fillet
200 g (7 oz) boneless, skinless trout or salmon fillet
300 g (10 oz) cooked shrimp, lobster or crab claws
1 onion
3 tomatoes
2 garlic cloves
3 ½ tablespoons oil
1 ⅓ liter (6 ¼ cups) fish stock
1 herb bouquet (parsley, thyme, bay leaf, leek, celery stalk)
grated zest of ½ orange
pinch saffron
salt and pepper
2 tablespoons minced parsley

A soup is only as good as the stock that goes into it, so be sure to have good fish stock on hand. Cut the fish into chunks and shell most of the shrimp. Cut onion and tomatoes into thin wedges and mince the garlic. Sauté onion, tomatoes and garlic in oil. Add stock, fish, herbs and zest, and simmer until the fish is cooked through. Add saffron, salt and pepper. Add the shrimp and heat through. Sprinkle with parsley. For an elegant touch, garnish with lobster or crab claws. Serve with garlic bread.

Bouillabaisse à la norvegienne

Coarsely ground fish

4 servings

500 g (1 1b) pollock, salmon, herring or mackerel
fillet
1 teaspoon salt
1 – 1 ½ dl (½-⅔ cup) milk
1 tablespoon potato starch
½ teaspoon pepper
seasonings

This mixture can be made in a food processor
and used for burgers.

Cut the fish into chunks and place in a food
processor with the salt. Pulse until evenly
chopped. This takes seconds. Add ⅓ of the milk
at a time, processing between each addition until
the mixture is smooth. Add potato starch and
seasonings at the end. Fry a trial patty and season to taste.

Seasoning suggestions

Minced parsley, chives, thyme, basil, tarragon,
grated fresh ginger, one or a blend of two or
more. Or minced onion, leek, bell pepper, chili or
other vegetables, preferably with one or two
herbs. Do not combine too many flavors at once.

Finely ground fish

1 kg (2 ¼ lb) boneless, skinless fillets of haddock,
cod, whiting or other white fish
25 g (1 ¼ tablespoons) salt
7 dl (scant 3 cups) ice-cold milk
25 g (2 tablespoons) potato starch
¼ teaspoon grated nutmeg

This smooth white forcemeat can be made into
fish patties, quenelles or fish pudding. Cut the
fish into strips and place in a food processor with
the salt. Pulse for a few seconds until elastic.
Gradually add milk, then starch and nutmeg.
Make and fry a trial cake. Adjust the seasoning, if
necessary.

For quenelles, heat 1 liter (4 cups) water and 2
teaspoons salt to a boil, or use fish stock. Form
small dumplings with a spoon and carefully place
in the water. Let simmer for 6 minutes, until the
quenelles float. Remove with a slotted spoon.
The remaining cooking water can be used in
sauce.

Fish quenelles *in curry sauce*

4 servings

2 onions, minced
1 garlic clove, minced
1 tablespoon butter
2 teaspoons curry powder
1 tablespoon flour
3 dl (1 ¼ cups) milk
1 dl (⅓ cup) fish stock or liquid from canned fish
quenelles
500 g (1 lb) fish quenelles
salt and pepper

Sauté onion and garlic in butter until shiny. Stir in
the curry and let cook for a few minutes. Stir in
the flour. Whisk in the milk and stock and heat to
boiling, whisking constantly. Let simmer for a
couple of minutes. Add the quenelles and heat
through. Season to taste. Serve with rice and
broccoli.

Fish quenelles in curry sauce

Oriental fish quenelles

4 servings

1 tablespoon butter
2 teaspoons curry powder
1 tablespoon flour
3 dl (1 ¼ cups) milk
1 dl (⅓ cup) fish stock or liquid from canned fish
quenelles
2-3 celery stalks, in 2 ½ cm (1") chunks
1 small can pineapple chunks
500 g (1 lb) fish quenelles
1 dl (⅓ cup) raisins
½ dl (3 tablespoons) unsalted peanuts

Melt the butter, stir in the curry and let cook for a couple of minutes. Stir in the flour. Whisk in the milk and stock and heat to boiling, whisking constantly. Let simmer for a couple of minutes. Add celery and pineapple and return to boiling. Add the quenelles and heat through. Stir in raisins and peanuts just before serving. Serve with rice and broccoli.

Mackerel patties

with mushroom-tomato compote
4 servings

600 g (1 ⅓ lb) mackerel fillets

Mushroom-tomato compote
1 onion, minced
50 g (2 oz) bacon, finely diced
2 tablespoons butter
8 fresh mushrooms, thinly sliced

3 tomatoes, peeled, seeded and chopped
1 tablespoon minced chives
salt and pepper

Prepare coarsely ground fish according to the recipe on page 54 and fry in butter. Fry onion and bacon in butter over low heat for 2-3 minutes. Add the mushrooms and sauté until shiny. Add tomato and chives and season with salt and pepper. Serve with the fish patties with sour cream on the side.

Herring patties

4 servings

750 g (1 ²/₃ lb) fresh herring fillets
2 teaspoons salt
1 ¹/₂ dl (²/₃ cup) milk
2 tablespoons potato starch
1 onion, chopped
3 tablespoons minced parsley
¹/₂ teaspoon pepper

Prepare coarsely ground fish according to the recipe on page 54. Add onion, parsley and pepper. Form into 4 or 8 flat patties and fry in butter over medium heat until golden brown. Serve the patties on whole grain bread or in pita or hamburger buns with dressing and lettuce.

Herring patties can also be served with fried onions, boiled potatoes, sour cream, pickled beats and grated carrots and apples.

Blandabaill

Blandabaill
6 servings

1 kg (2 ¼ lb) boneless, skinless fresh haddock fillet
2 onions, in wedges
1 liter (4 cups) peeled potato chunks
2 tablespoons salt
1 dl (⅓ cup) milk
3 tablespoons potato starch
1 tablespoon flour
150 g (5 oz) bacon, diced

Grind the fish once with onion, potatoes and salt. Gradually stir in the milk. Add the starch and flour, mixing well. Make large balls and put a piece of bacon in each ball. Simmer in salted water (½ teaspoon salt per liter/quart) until cooked through, around 20 minutes. Serve with boiled carrots, fried bacon cubes and potatoes.

Hitraball

Hitraball
4 servings

500 g (1 lb) boneless, skinless haddock fillet
1 teaspoon salt
3-5 dl (1 ¼-2 cups) 2% milk
1 ½ tablespoons potato starch
½ onion, minced
75 g (3 oz) suet, diced
5-8 dl (2-3 cups) fish stock

Prepare finely ground fish according to the recipe on page 54. Add onions and form into large balls. Place a suet cube in each ball. Let simmer in good fish stock for 15-20 minutes. Serve with boiled potatoes, fried bacon and rutabagas.

Dried salted fish

Norwegian klippfish is cod (or other members of the cod family) that has been salted and dried in a special process. Treated in this way, the fish retains its flavor and nutrients – only the water is removed. It is healthy, tasty and it keeps well – a truly natural product. It is sold in many grocery stores and specialty shops, either whole or in pieces, loose or prepackaged. In Norway, some stores sell it pre-soaked and cleaned, frozen or refrigerated.

Cleaning and soaking
Cut the fish into smaller pieces. Remove the skin, which is easy with dried fish, so soaking doesn't take so long. Soak the fish in lots of cold water for 24-72 hours, changing water once a day. The larger and thicker the fish, the longer it needs to soak. If the fish is thick (5-6 cm/2-2 1/4 "), it should be soaked for 72 hours. Fish that will be fried needs to be soaked longer than fish that will be poached. If you are uncertain, you can taste a little piece from the thickest part of the fish. Cook a piece for 5 minutes. It should have a mildly salty flavor. Salt fish that has been soaked can be frozen for later use. It's a good idea to soak a large amount and freeze it down. Then if you get the urge for bacalao, it's easy to prepare.

Estimating portions
1 kg (2 1/4 lb) dried salted fish corresponds to 1 1/2 kg (3 lb) soaked. After cleaning, there should be around 1 kg (2 1/4 lb) ready to cook fish. When buying klippfish, count on 100-150 g (3 1/2 - 5 oz) dried salted fish per person.

Bacalao à la viscaina
4 servings

700 g (1 1/2 lb) soaked and cleaned klippfish
1 dl (1/3 cup) olive oil
4 onions, sliced or diced
2 tablespoons tomato paste
6 tomatoes, sliced (or same amount canned)
6 potatoes, sliced
2 red or green bell peppers, sliced
1/2 red or green chili, minced (or 1/2 teaspoon cayenne pepper)

Cut the fish into 4 cm (1 1/2") pieces. Heat the oil in a heavy pot. Sauté the onion until shiny and stir in the tomato puree. Layer all ingredients in the sauce. Heat to boiling, lower the heat, and let simmer over low heat until all ingredient are cooked, around one hour.

Red pollock

Salt fish

Red pollock
4 servings

600 g (1 ¹/₃ lb) red pollock

Soak the fish in cold water for 4-5 hours. Clean and cut into serving pieces. Place in a pot with water to cover. Heat to boiling. Drain. Heat new water to boiling, add the fish and let simmer for around 10 minutes. Serve with boiled potatoes and mashed root vegetables (page 118). Creamed peas, fried bacon, boiled potatoes and flatbread are traditional side dishes.

Lightly salted redfish
4 servings

³/₄-1 kg (1 ³/₄ - 2 ¹/₄ lb) lightly salted redfish

Cut the fish into serving pieces. Heat the water to boiling and add the fish. Let simmer for 8-10 minutes, until the fish separates from the bone. Serve with boiled potatoes and creamed carrots (page 118). Cooked vegetables and béchamel sauce or egg butter with chopped parsley is also good with lightly salted redfish.

Lightly salted redfish

Salt herring *and new potatoes*
4 servings

4-6 salt herring fillets
8-12 new potatoes, cooked
1 onion, thinly sliced
1 dl (½ cup) diced pickled beets

Cut the herring fillets into wide strips on the diagonal. Cut the potatoes into thick slices. Arrange herring, onion, potatoes and beets on a platter and serve with flatbread and dairy sour cream.

Dried fish

Dried fish has to be soaked before cooking.
During the drying process, around 70% of the
water is removed. Some of that has to be re-
placed before cooking. Soak the fish in lots of
cold water. It is important to keep the fish cold,
4°C (40°F) or colder. Split or filleted dried fish
needs only half the soaking time of whole fish.
Remove skin and bones after soaking but before
cooking. For a casual dinner, leave the skin and
bones on and let everyone clean their chunks of
fish at the table.

Dried fish *Mediterranean style*

600 g (1 ¹/₃ lb) soaked and cleaned dried fish
4 potatoes, peeled and cut into wedges
1-2 tomatoes, peeled, seeded and diced
1 dl (¹/₃ cup) olive oil
juice of 2 oranges
1 teaspoon salt
¹/₂ teaspoon pepper
chopped parsley

Cut the fish into 5 cm (2") pieces and let simmer,
covered, for 10 minutes. Add the potatoes, cover
and cook for 15 minutes more. Add the remaining ingredients, cover and shake a few times.
Garnish with chopped parsley.

Lutefisk

4 servings

3 kg (6 ½ lb) lutefisk
2-3 tablespoons salt
coarsely ground pepper

Lutefisk is best cooked without adding water in the oven. Preheat the oven to 200°C (400°F). Place the fish, skin down, in an ovenproof dish. Sprinkle with salt and pepper. Cover with aluminum foil and bake in the middle of the oven for around 40 minutes. Check for doneness after 30 minutes. A smaller amount of fish should cook in less time. Count on 15 minutes per kilo (2 ¼ lb) fish. Remember that the temperature of the fish when it is placed in the oven determines the cooking time. Large cold pieces take longer to cook than small pieces at room temperature. Serve lutefisk piping hot on heated plates with creamed peas, boiled potatoes and crisp diced bacon with bacon fat. Place coarse salt, a pepper mill, lefse and mustard on the table. According to tradition, cold beer and aquavit are the best accompaniments. Other alternatives are light beer or lemonade.

Helpful hint
Do you like firm *lutefisk*? Sprinkle with salt and refrigerate for 2 hours. Pour off any liquid, then rinse the fish with cold water. Cook without salt.

Fermented fish *from Valdres*

3 kg (6 ½ lb) fresh mountain trout of the highest quality
200 g (1 ½ dl) coarse sea salt
1 tablespoon sugar

Clean and rinse the fish in lots of cold water. Do not let it come into contact with the ground (any dirt or earth). Dry well and sprinkle a little salt in the belly of each fish. Arrange the fish, belly slightly up, on the diagonal, in a well-scrubbed, clean wooden barrel. Sprinkle salt over, under, and between the fish in the barrel. Place a weight on the fish and let it rest at room temperature for 24 hours, then move it to a cold cellar. After 2-3 days, brine will form. If the brine does not cover the fish, make some brine and add it. Cook brine with 3 liter (quarts) water, 1 dl (scant ½ cup) salt and 2 teaspoons sugar. Let the brine cool completely before adding to the fish. The fish is ready after 5-6 weeks. If mold forms, pour off all the brine and make new. Sometimes the finished fish is so ripe that it can be spread with a knife. Serve with boiled potatoes, butter and flatbread, or sour cream and red onions.

Smoked salmon/trout with apple salad

Smoked salmon/trout
with apple salad
4 servings

2 sweet red apples
2 tablespoons vinaigrette
½ head oak leaf lettuce
200 g (8 oz) smoked salmon or trout

Vinaigrette
1 tablespoon wine vinegar
½ teaspoon Dijon mustard
1 teaspoon clear honey
1 small garlic clove, minced
3 tablespoons olive oil
salt and pepper

Make the dressing first. Combine all ingredients in a jar with a tight-fitting lid. Shake until emulsified. Cut the apples into thin wedges. Toss apples with dressing. Divide lettuce among four plates. Top with apples. Cut fish into thin slices and arrange with the apples.

Smoked mackerel snack

4 servings

400 g (14 oz) warm-smoked mackerel
400 g (14 oz) pepper-smoked mackerel
400 g (14 oz) cold-smoked mackerel
6 eggs
chopped scallions
butter
lettuce
bell pepper rings
celery stalks, in chunks

Clean and fillet the fish. Cut the warm and pepper-smoked mackerel into medium-thick slices. Cut the cold-smoked mackerel into very thin slices. Scramble the eggs with chopped scallions in butter. Arrange fish and eggs on a platter with the fresh vegetables. Serve with whole grain bread, butter and sour cream.

Mollusks

Preparation of live mollusks

Fresh live mollusks should close their shells when tapped. Open shells are dead and should be discarded. Remember that mollusks are live animals and should not be frozen raw. Cooked mollusk meat freezes very well. Mollusks that remain closed after cooking should also be discarded. All varieties of scallops are an exception and can be frozen once out of the shell.

Basic recipe for mussels
1 serving

1 kg (2 ¼ lb) Norwegian farmed mussels
½ small onion, chopped
5 cm (2") leek, chopped
½ celery stalk, chopped
1 tablespoon butter or olive oil

Place all ingredients in a pot. Cover and cook at high heat for 3-4 minutes. Shake the pot several times so that the bottom shells rise to the top and the top shells fall to the bottom. Cook for 3-4 minutes more, until all the shells have opened.

Mussels in white wine
1 serving

Mussels au gratin

1 kg (2 ¼ lb) mussels prepared according to basic recipe
2 dl (¾ cup) dry white wine
2 garlic cloves, minced
2 tablespoons minced parsley

Prepare according to basic recipe. When the shells have opened, add wine and garlic. Shake, reheat to boiling, sprinkle with parsley and serve immediately.

Mussels au gratin
Remove the empty half of each mussel. Place the remaining shells with the meat in a large oven-proof dish or on a baking sheet. Sprinkle with chopped chives, parsley, garlic, coarsely ground pepper and grated cheese. Bake for a few minutes in a hot oven or place under the grill for 3-4 minutes.

Mussels in white wine

Marinated shrimp

with couscous and grilled vegetables

1 eggplant
1 zucchini
1 red bell pepper
1 ½ dl (⅔ cup) olive oil
salt and pepper
200 g (7 oz) couscous
1 tablespoon chopped fresh mint
350 g (13 oz) shelled cooked shrimp
juice of 1 lime
juice of 3 lemons
1 tablespoon chopped coriander
1 lime, sliced

Slice the eggplant and zucchini. Cut the pepper into strips. Brush with some of the oil and grill on both sides. Cut the vegetables into 2 cm (¾") squares and season with salt and pepper. Prepare couscous according to package directions. Stir in the mint. Combine the shrimp and remaining ingredients. Arrange couscous in the bottom of a platter. Top with grilled vegetables and marinated shrimp. Garnish with lime slices. Use the shrimp marinade as dressing for the salad.

Crab

4 servings

4 crabs
French bread
butter
mayonnaise
2 lemons
vinegar
pepper

If you buy live crabs, prepare according to the directions under. The crabs can be served as they are, or you can make it easier for your guests by cleaning them before serving. Remove and discard the sac behind the eyes and the gills. Crack the claws with a nutcracker. Put the crab back together before serving. Some of the fun of eating crab is to work a little for the food. Serve with bread, butter and mayonnaise. Garnish with lemon wedges, vinegar and place the pepper grinder on the table. You can also serve it with chili sauce.

Chili sauce

4 servings

1 dl (½ cup) dairy sour cream
½ dl (¼ cup) mayonnaise
½ dl (¼ cup) tomato-based chili sauce
1 tablespoon lemon juice
½ teaspoon mustard
½ teaspoon Worcestershire sauce
sugar

Combine all ingredients and season to taste with sugar.

Preparing crab

Heat a large pot of salted water (50 g/2 ½ tablespoons salt per liter) to boiling. Add the live crabs, a couple at a time, to the rapidly boiling water. Do not add too many at once, as the water temperature will go down too much. Cover and reheat to boiling. Lower the heat and let simmer until done. Cooking time for crabs is 15 minutes for the first 500 g (1 lb) and then 10 minutes for the next 500 g (1 lb). A crab is finished cooking when the small claws can be pulled out easily. Remove from the cooking liquid and let the crabs cool belly up, to prevent the juices from running off. Boiled crabs are best eaten warm or when refrigerated for no more than 24 hours after cooking. Cooked crabs freeze well.

White meat

Marinades

Shredded meat should be marinated from 30 minutes to 3 hours. Whole pieces can be marinated overnight, covered and refrigerated. Do not add salt if the chicken is going to be marinated for a long time, as salt draws out liquid. It's better to salt the meat after cooking. Combine all marinade ingredients in a plastic bag. Add the chicken parts and knot. Turn the bag several times to redistribute the marinade.

Red wine marinade

3 dl (1 ¼ cups) red wine
3 ½ tablespoons oil
1 garlic clove, minced
½ teaspoon salt
1 tablespoon sugar
4 white peppercorns, crushed
1 teaspoon dried thyme
2 bay leaves, crumbled

Herb marinade

1 ½ dl (⅔ cup) oil
2 tablespoons wine vinegar
3 tablespoons chopped fresh herbs (tarragon, thyme, basil and rosemary)
1 teaspoon salt
freshly ground pepper
1 garlic clove, minced

Tandoori marinade

2 ½ dl (1 cup) natural yogurt
3 garlic cloves, minced
2 tablespoons grated fresh ginger
2 teaspoons garam masala

2 teaspoons salt
1 teaspoon chili powder
1 teaspoon ground paprika

Quick chicken and rice
3-4 servings

3 dl (1 ¼ cups) rice
2 onions, in wedges
3 tablespoons oil
7 dl (3 cups) chicken stock (1 ½ cubes + water)
1 grilled or roasted chicken
1 package frozen vegetables (or same amount fresh)
1 small can corn

Quick chicken and rice

Sauté rice and onion in oil in a pot. Add the stock and heat to boiling. Cover and lower heat. Cut the chicken into small pieces and place on the rice. Pour over the vegetables. Let simmer for around 15 minutes, until the rice is cooked and the chicken and vegetables are warm. Serve with crusty bread.

Roast chicken with herb sauce

Roast chicken *with herb sauce*

1 chicken, around 1 kg (2 ¼ lb)
2 tablespoons lemon juice
2 tablespoons brown sugar
1 tablespoon honey
1 garlic clove, minced
3 ½ tablespoons soy sauce

Preheat the oven to 180-200°C (350-400°F). Truss the chicken. Combine the remaining ingredients and brush onto the chicken. Roast for 1¼ hours, brushing with the mixture a couple of times during roasting. Let the chicken rest for 10-15 minutes before carving. Serve with rice and herb sauce.

Helpful hint:

Cut small slits in the skin over the breast and insert thin slices of garlic and herbs.

Green herb sauce

2 dl (1 cup) peas
4-5 dl (2 cups) fresh spinach leaves
butter
1 dl (½ cup) chicken stock
1 ½ dl (¾ cup) milk
3 tablespoons chopped fresh herbs (such as coriander or basil)
3-4 tablespoons crème fraiche (or dairy sour cream)
salt and freshly ground pepper
2 tablespoons cold butter

Sauté the peas and spinach in a little butter for a few seconds. Add stock and milk and heat to boiling. Pour into a blender, add the herbs and puree until smooth. Whisk in the crème fraiche. Return to the saucepan, reheat carefully and season with salt and pepper. Beat in cold butter at the end for a shiny, thick sauce

Chicken with 40 cloves of garlic

This is a classic dish. Do not be afraid of all the garlic. It becomes mild and flavorful after cooking.

4 servings

1 chicken, around 1 kg (2 ¼ lb)
40 garlic cloves, unpeeled
1 small bunch parsley (preferably flat leaf) and other herbs
olive oil
salt and freshly ground pepper
a little grated lemon zest
around 1 dl (1/2 cup) dry white wine

Preheat the oven to 200°C (400°F). Place a few garlic cloves and half the herbs inside the chicken. Truss. Brush with oil and sprinkle with salt and pepper. Place in an ovenproof dish. Sprinkle with lemon zest and arrange the rest of the garlic and herbs around the chicken. Pour the wine into the bottom of the dish and cover with aluminum foil. Bake for around 45 minutes. Remove the foil, increase the temperature to 225°C (425°F) and bake for 20-30 more minutes. Strain the pan juices. Serve with bread, salad and pan juices.

Helpful hint

Slit the garlic and press out the contents. Mash to a paste, add a little chopped herbs and season with salt and pepper. Delicious on fresh bread or toast.

Chicken with 40 cloves of garlic

Combine mayonnaise, mustard sauce and crème fraiche and season with lemon juice, salt and pepper in a bowl. Add the remaining ingredients and toss.

This salad is also good with plain grilled chicken legs.

Oven-fried chicken legs
4-6 servings

1 egg
1 ½ tablespoons sesame seeds
2 tablespoons fine breadcrumbs
3 tablespoons grated parmesan cheese
½ teaspoon ground paprika
salt and pepper
8 chicken legs

Preheat the oven to 200°C (400°F). Beat the egg. Combine the sesame seeds, crumbs, cheese and paprika. Dip the chicken in egg, then coat with the sesame seed mixture. Arrange in a greased ovenproof dish and bake for around 50 minutes. Serve with avocado salad and bread.

Avocado salad
2 tablespoons mayonnaise
1 tablespoon mustard sauce
3 tablespoons crème fraiche or dairy sour cream
2 tablespoons lemon juice
salt and pepper
2 tomatoes, peeled, seeded and chopped
2 avocados, peeled, pitted and cubed
1 garlic clove, grated
½ red chili, minced
3 tablespoons fresh chopped coriander

Sweet-and-sour chicken
3 servings

3 boneless, skinless chicken breasts
1 garlic clove, minced
1 tablespoon grated fresh ginger
oil
½ bell pepper, in strips
10-15 string beans
1 can (6-8 oz) pineapple chunks in juice, drained (reserve the juice)
½ leek, sliced

Sweet-and-sour sauce
3 tablespoons soy sauce
1 dl (½ cup) pineapple juice (from the canned pineapple)
1 dl (½ cup) chicken stock
2-3 tablespoons tomato paste
1-2 teaspoons cornstarch stirred into
2 teaspoons cold water
1 tablespoon wine vinegar
1 tablespoon sugar

Cut the chicken into thin strips and sauté with garlic and ginger in oil in a wok or large pan until the meat turns white. Add pepper, beans, pineapple and leek. Stir-fry for a few minutes until vegetables begin to soften slightly. Combine soy sauce, pineapple juice, stock, tomato paste and cornstarch mixture and pour over the meat. Heat to boiling. Season with vinegar and sugar. Serve with rice.

Sweet-and-sour chicken

Chicken with shrimp pasta
2 servings

2 boneless, skinless chicken breasts
salt and ground pepper
1 teaspoon minced red chili
1 teaspoon grated fresh ginger
oil

Sprinkle the chicken with salt, pepper, chili and ginger. Sauté in butter for 3-4 minutes per side. Let rest for a minute or two.

1 garlic clove, minced
2 ½ dl (1 cup) béchamel sauce

3 dl (1¼ cups) cooked corkscrew pasta
salt and ground pepper
100 g (4 oz) cooked, shelled shrimp, chopped
1 tablespoon chopped fresh herbs

Sauté the garlic with the butter when making the béchamel sauce. Stir into the pasta and season with salt and pepper. Top with shrimp and sprinkle with herbs. Serve with chicken and fresh asparagus.

Chicken in pastry

with apricot sauce.
4 servings

6 boneless, skinless chicken breasts
salt
2 tablespoons minced shallots
1 teaspoon minced red chili
1 teaspoon grated fresh ginger
1-2 tablespoons chopped fresh tarragon or 1
teaspoon dried
2 eggs
1 dl (scant ½ cup) whipping cream
freshly ground pepper
butter
4 puff pastry sheets (US: 1 package frozen puff
pastry, defrosted)

Cut 2 of the chicken breasts into chunks and
place in a food processor. Add a little salt and
pulse several times. Add shallot, chili, ginger, 1
egg and cream and process until well mixed.
Season with ground pepper. Sprinkle the remaining chicken breasts with salt and pepper and
sauté in butter for 2 ½ minutes per side. Let cool.
Preheat the oven to 225°C (425°F). (US: Divide
the puff pastry into 4 pieces of equal size.) Roll
the puff pastry to 3 mm thick. Halve each chicken
breast lengthwise, but do not cut all the way
through. It should open like a book. Fill with the
chopped chicken mixture and fold over. Lightly
beat the remaining egg. Place a stuffed chicken
breast on each sheet of puff pastry. Brush around
the edges of the pastry with beaten egg. Fold
over the pastry, pressing the edges lightly together with a fork. Place the "packets" on a greased
oven sheet and bake on the center shelf for
around 15 minutes, until golden. Serve with apricot sauce.

Apricot sauce
2 onions, chopped

2 garlic cloves, minced
oil
2 bay leaves, crumbled
3 tablespoons curry powder
1 can (14 oz) apricots, drained and chopped
¾ dl (½ cup) apple juice or apricot nectar
2 dl (1 cup) chicken stock
2 dl (1 cup) light cream
2 dl (1 cup) crème fraiche or dairy sour cream
1 teaspoon cornstarch stirred into 1 teaspoon
cold water
salt and pepper

Fry onion and garlic in oil with the bay leaves and
curry powder over low heat for around 10 minutes. Add the remaining ingredients and simmer
for a few minutes. Let cool slightly. Pour into a
blender and puree until smooth. Strain into a
clean saucepan. If too thin, add cornstarch mixture and simmer until thickened. Season with salt
and pepper. If using sour cream, stir in now, then
reheat, but do not allow to boil.

Roast turkey
– with or without stuffing

500 g (1 lb) per person
butter
salt and pepper

Defrost the turkey in the refrigerator (it should
take 2-3 days). Remove the bag of giblets. Make
stock for the gravy: Remove the fat and bloody
bits from the giblets. Reserve the liver for another
dish. Brown the giblets in butter, add cold water
to cover and let simmer for 1-2 hours. Preheat
the oven to 160°C (325°F). Fold the wing tips
under back, so that the bird lies on them while
roasting. Remove any bloody bits from the inside
of the bird. Fill with desired "stuffing" (see following recipes) and close the opening with skewers
or sew with cotton thread. Tie the legs together.
Roast for 30 minutes per kilo (15 minutes per lb)
plus 30-45 minutes, if filled with a raw stuffing.
After 30 minutes roasting, add 5 dl (2 cups) hot
water with 1 teaspoon chicken bouillon powder
to the pan (add more later, if necessary). Baste
with cooking juices several times during roasting.
Let the turkey rest for 15-20 minutes before carving. Serve with potatoes, vegetables and cream
sauce.

Walnut stuffing with dried fruit
1 onion
300 g (5-6 slices) white bread, crusts removed
butter
150 g (5 oz) walnuts
100 g (3 ½ oz) dried apricots
75 g (2 oz) dried figs
75 g (3 oz) prunes
1 apple
2 eggs
1 teaspoon salt
½ teaspoon pepper

Mince the onion, cube the bread and sauté in
butter until the bread is golden brown. Transfer
to a large bowl. Chop the walnuts, shred the
dried fruit and grate the apple. Stir into the bread
cubes. Whisk in the egg. The stuffing can either
be spooned into the turkey or it can be baked in
an ovenproof dish for the last 30-40 minutes of
roasting time.

Sausage stuffing
500 g (1 lb) loose turkey sausage
1 onion, minced
1 red or green bell pepper, diced
turkey liver, diced

Combine all ingredients. Spoon into the turkey.
It should be no more than ¾ full, as the stuffing
expands during roasting. Count on 30-45 minutes longer cooking time when using this
stuffing. The stuffing "stretches" the turkey.

Cream sauce
10 servings

1 ½ liter (6 cups) turkey stock (+ chicken stock,
if necessary)
1 ½ dl (²⁄₃ cup) flour
2 dl (1 cup) water
2 dl (1 cup) whipping cream
2 tablespoons port wine or red currant jelly
4 tablespoons (¼ cup) soy sauce
salt and ground pepper

Measure the giblet stock, adding chicken stock if
necessary. Heat to boiling. Place the flour and
water in a jar. Tighten the lid and shake to blend.
Whisk into the boiling stock. Let simmer for
around 5 minutes. Add the remaining ingredients. Be sure to deglaze the turkey roasting pan
with water, reheat, scraping the bottom, and add
the juices to the sauce for more flavor.

Honey-sesame glazed turkey breast

4-6 servings

1 turkey breast, around 1 kg (2 ¼ lb)
1 teaspoon salt
ground pepper
2 tablespoons butter
2 dl (1 cup) white wine or cider
1 dl (½ cup) chicken stock
3 tablespoons melted honey
3 tablespoons soy sauce
1 garlic clove, minced
2 tablespoons sesame seeds

Honey-sesame glazed turkey breast

Preheat the oven to 180°C (350°F). Sprinkle the turkey with salt and pepper and brown in butter on all sides in a pan that tolerates oven heat. Add wine and stock and roast for around 30 minutes. Remove from the oven and pour off (and reserve) any cooking juices. Increase the heat to 225°C (425°F). Combine honey, soy sauce and garlic and brush onto the meat. Roast for 5 minutes. Brush the meat one more time and sprinkle with sesame seed. Roast for 5 minutes more. Let the meat rest for around 15 minutes. Carve and served with potatoes, orange sauce, steamed early cabbage, turnips and snow peas.

Orange sauce
2 shallots
1 tablespoon butter
1 teaspoon chopped red chili

2 dl (1 cup) strained cooking juices or stock and white wine
2 dl (1 cup) orange juice, strained
2 dl (1 cup) crème fraiche or dairy sour cream
grated orange zest
1/2 teaspoon salt
freshly ground white pepper

Mince the shallots and sauté in butter until shiny. Add the chili, cooking juices and orange juice and let simmer for around 10 minutes. Add crème fraiche and simmer a few minutes more. If using sour cream, reheat, but do not allow to boil. Season with orange zest, salt and pepper.

Peppered turkey

Peppered turkey

turkey breast slices, around 150 g (5 oz) per person
ground pepper mix (white, black, green and rose)
salt
butter

Dip the turkey into the pepper mix. Sprinkle with salt and sauté in butter for 2-3 minutes per side. Let the meat rest for a few minutes before serving. Serve with potato salad and tarragon sauce.

Potato salad with honey dressing

1 kg (2 1/4 lb) tiny potatoes (new potatoes)
1 endive
200 g (8 oz) mixed greens
2 yellow bell peppers
1 red onion, thinly sliced
chopped chives

Honey dressing

2 tablespoons honey
3 1/2 tablespoons white wine vinegar
1 1/2 teaspoons salt
1 dl (scant 1/2 cup) safflower oil

grated zest of 1 lemon
freshly ground pepper

Place the endive in cold water to retain crispness. Rinse the greens. Halve potatoes, slice large ones. Combine all ingredients in a bowl. Place all dressing ingredients in a jar, screw on the lid and shake. Pour over the salad.

Tarragon sauce

2 tablespoons butter
1 package béarnaise sauce mix
2 dl (1 cup) white wine
1 1/2 dl (2/3 cup) light cream
1 egg yolk
2 tablespoons chopped tarragon

Melt the butter and add the sauce mix, wine and cream. Let simmer for a few minutes. Remove the saucepan from the heat and whisk in the egg yolk and tarragon. Serve immediately. Do not boil after the egg yolk is added or mixture may separate.

Turkey burgers

4-6 burgers

400 g (14 oz) ground turkey
1 teaspoon salt
½ teaspoon pepper
½ onion, minced
1 tablespoon potato starch
1 egg
3 ½ tablespoons water
rosemary, oregano, garlic, chili or other spices
butter

Combine all ingredients in a bowl. Form into 4 or 6 round patties. Fry two at a time in butter over medium heat for 3-4 minutes per side, until cooked through. Serve with fried potatoes and a salad.

Helpful hint
For extra flavor, add chopped pickle, beets or grated carrot to the ground meat.

Chicken fricassee

6-8 servings

meat from 2 poached hens
6 carrots
1 large leek
2 parsley roots
1 celeriac

5 tablespoons (1/3 cup) butter
1¼ dl (½ cup) flour
1 ½ liter (6 cups) chicken stock or cooking liquid from the hens
½-1 dl (⅓ cup) whipping cream
lemon juice
salt and pepper
chopped parsley

Cut the meat into serving pieces. Peel and cut the vegetables into 1 cm (½") chunks. In a pot, melt the butter and stir in the flour. Let cook slightly. Heat the stock to boiling. Whisk in the boiling stock and add the cream, chicken and vegetables. Let simmer until the vegetables are tender, 10-15 minutes. Season with lemon juice, salt and pepper. Sprinkle with parsley and serve with boiled potatoes.

Helpful hint
If you don't have time to poach hens for the fricassee, you can make it with chicken, which take less time to cook. You can even simmer boneless, skinless chicken breasts in a good chicken stock with vegetables and make sauce from the stock. Fricassee in a flash!

Turkey stew

4 servings

600 g (1 ⅓ lb) turkey strips
butter
8 tiny onions
200 g (7 oz) mushrooms
5 dl (2 cups) chicken stock
½ teaspoon dry mustard
½ teaspoon ground paprika
1 tablespoon Worcestershire sauce
salt and pepper
3 tablespoons tomato paste
pinch sugar
3 dl (1 ¼ cups) sour cream or whipping cream
1 green and 1 red bell pepper, in strips
chopped parsley

Brown the turkey in butter. Transfer to a pot.
Chop the onions and quarter the mushrooms and
sauté lightly. Add to the pot with the stock and
the other ingredients. Let simmer for a few minutes. Served rice or mashed potatoes with beets
and pickles.

Chicken fricassee

Turkey stew

Chicken in red wine sauce

4-5 servings

1 large chicken, around 1 ½ kg (3 ¼ lb)

3 ¾ dl (1 2/3 cups) red wine

2 garlic cloves, minced

1 bay leaf

2 tablespoons chopped fresh thyme or

1 teaspoon dried

100 g (3 ½ oz) salt pork

1 ½ teaspoons salt

¾ teaspoon white pepper

4 tablespoons (¼ cup) cognac (optional)

chicken stock

1 tablespoon tomato paste (optional)

around 20 tiny onions

250 g (8 oz) mushrooms

1 ½ tablespoons butter

1 tablespoon flour

fresh thyme

Cut the chicken into 8 pieces. Combine the wine, garlic, bay leaf and thyme in a bowl and add the chicken. Refrigerate overnight or let

Mrinate at room temperature for 4-5 hours. Remove the chicken and dry well. Pour the marinade into a pot and heat to boiling. Dice the salt pork and fry until all the fat has melted. Transfer the pork to the pot but leave the fat in the pan. Sprinkle the chicken with salt and pepper and brown in the fat. Pour over the cognac and ignite. When the flames have died down on their own, transfer the chicken to the pot. Add enough stock to just cover the chicken. Add tomato paste for more color, if desired. Simmer over low heat for around 40 minutes, until tender. While the chicken is cooking, sauté the onions and mushrooms and add to the pot. Knead the butter and flour together and whisk into the pot to thicken the sauce. Let simmer for 5 more minutes. Adjust the seasoning. Garnish with fresh thyme. Serve with potatoes, rice or bread.

Making stock

You can't make good soups and sauces without good stock! Stock is not as time- consuming to make as many think – and it's worth the effort. Make a lot and freeze it in small containers.

Chicken and hen carcasses, backs, wings and trimmings are perfect for cooking stock. Brown in butter with chopped carrot, celeriac, onion and leek. Add cold water to just cover. Heat to boiling, skimming frequently for a clear stock. Add salt, peppercorns, bay leaf and a parsley sprig. Let simmer for 1 hour or more. Strain.

Curried chicken soup

4 servings

²/₃ dl (¹/₄ cup) lentils
2-3 onions
2 teaspoons curry powder
butter
1 liter (4 cups) chicken stock
1-2 dl (¹/₂-³/₄ cup) whipping cream
1 small can (²/₃ cup) coconut milk
skinless and boneless meat from 1 poached hen or chicken
salt and pepper

Cook lentils according to package directions. Mince the onion and sauté with the curry powder in butter until shiny. Add stock, cream and coconut milk. Simmer until thickened. Cut the meat into bite-size pieces and add. Season with salt and pepper. For a more hearty soup, add cooked rice just before serving and heat through.

Meat

Marinades

All roasts can be marinated before cooking. The purpose of marinating is to add flavor to the meat, but marinating can also help to tenderize meat. Acidic liquids, such as vinegar, wine, lemon juice, buttermilk and yogurt are used. The acid starts the tenderizing process and helps the meat to stay fresh longer. Since salt draws moisture from the meat, it should not be used in marinades. Small pieces of meat require shorter marinating time than large. If the meat is going to be browned that same day, you can leave the meat at room temperature. If it's going to be used the next day or later, it should be refrigerated.

It's a good idea to place the meat in a plastic bag. Add the marinade and press out the air before tying the bag together. To be safe, put the bag of meat into another plastic bag to make sure that it doesn't leak, or place the bag in a bowl. Rotate the bag every so often. By using a bag for marinating meat, you can be sure that the meat is covered in marinade, and there are fewer utensils to wash.

Red wine marinade
4 tablespoons red wine
1 garlic clove, minced
1 tablespoon dried rosemary
2 bay leaves

Combine all ingredients. Use with beef, lamb and pork.

Mint Marinade
1 dl (½ cup) olive oil
1 dl (½ cup) dry white wine (or apple juice)
⅔ dl (¼ cup) chopped fresh mint

Combine all ingredients. This marinade is especially good with lamb.

Honey marinade
2 tablespoons olive oil
1 tablespoon honey
2 tablespoons prepared mustard
2 garlic cloves, minced
2 teaspoons chopped fresh coriander
1 tablespoon lemon juice

Combine all ingredients. This marinade is especially good with pork and lamb.

Chili marinade
4 tablespoons (¼ cup) oil
1 teaspoon chili oil or 1 teaspoon minced red chili
½ onion, sliced
1 tablespoon chopped fresh oregano
½ teaspoon coarsely crushed peppercorns

Combine all ingredients. This marinade is especially good with beef and lamb.

Pork - from trimmed, lean products to pork ribs and chops.

Garlic marinade

4 tablespoons ($1/2$ cup) oil
2 teaspoons lemon juice or 1 tablespoon white
wine vinegar
2 garlic cloves, minced
3 peppercorns, crushed
1 teaspoon dried rosemary
1 parsley stalk, chopped
$1/2$ teaspoon dried thyme

Combine all ingredients. This marinade is especially good with lamb.

Herb marinade

3 $1/2$ tablespoons cognac
1 tablespoon oil
1 garlic clove, minced
1 teaspoon dried rosemary
$1/2$ teaspoon dried thyme
$1/4$ teaspoon dried basil
juice of $1/2$ lemon

Combine all ingredients. This marinade is especially good with beef and lamb.

Roast pork

with cider sauce and vegetables
8-10 servings

2 kg (4 ½ lb) boneless fresh ham, rind on
1 tablespoon salt
1 teaspoon pepper
2 carrots
2 onions
7 ½ dl (3 cups) water

Preheat the oven to 175°C (350°F). Rub the meat with salt and pepper. Insert a meat thermometer into the thickest part. Clean the vegetables and cut into chunks. Place in an oven tray with the meat. Roast until the internal temperature reaches 76°C (170°), 2 ½ –3 hours. Let the meat rest while preparing the side dishes. Just before serving, place under the grill to crisp the rind.

Cider sauce

6-8 servings

½ onion
1 leek
1 teaspoon oil
3 dl (1 ¼ cups) apple cider
6 dl (2 ½ cups) cooking liquid from roast
1 tablespoon cornstarch
3 ½ tablespoons cold water
1 teaspoon grated fresh ginger (or ½ teaspoon dried)
1 teaspoon lemon juice
½ teaspoon sugar

Finely chop the onion and leek and sauté in oil until soft and shiny. Add the cider and reduce by ⅔. Add the stock and reduce by ½. Stir the cornstarch into the water and whisk into the stock. Simmer until thickened. Season with ginger, lemon juice and sugar.

Vegetables

100 g (4 oz) snow peas
2 bell peppers, red and/or yellow
2 scallions
1 small broccoli stalk, parboiled for 1 minute, if desired.
1 tablespoon oil
½ teaspoon salt
½ teaspoon pepper

Halve the snow peas, cut the peppers into strips, the scallions into rings and the broccoli into florets. Sauté in oil for a few minutes over medium heat. Sprinkle with salt and pepper.

Helpful hints

Roast fresh ham can be served in many ways and with all kinds of accompaniments. Try these:
– Sautéed apple wedges, Brussels sprouts and crispy bacon shreds
– Exotic fruits and mango chutney
– Sauerkraut (page 118) and brown gravy

Roast lamb

6-8 servings

2 ½ kg (5 lb) leg of lamb or 1 ½-2 kg (3-4 ½ lb) rolled boneless leg of lamb

3 garlic cloves

2 teaspoons salt

½ teaspoon coarsely ground pepper

1 teaspoon dried rosemary

5 dl (2 cups) boiling water

1 kg (2 ¼ lb) potatoes

1 leek

3 parsley roots

2 carrots

1 garlic clove

2 tablespoons olive oil

1 teaspoon salt

½ teaspoon coarsely ground pepper

1 teaspoon herbs de Provence

Au jus sauce

5 dl (2 cups) cooking liquid from roast

1 ½ tablespoons cornstarch

2 tablespoons cold water

salt and pepper

Remove the tailbone with a small, sharp knife or buy a boned, rolled roast. Peel the garlic and cut into slivers. Make small slits in the meat and insert the garlic. Season with salt, pepper and rosemary. Insert a meat thermometer into the thickest part. It should not touch bone. Place in an oven tray and roast for around 2 hours, until the internal temperature reaches 65°C (150°F). After around 1 ½ hours, add the boiling water. Peel and clean the potatoes and vegetables. Cut into coarse chunks. Mince the garlic. Heat the olive oil in a cast iron pot and sauté the vegetables with the seasonings for around 5 minutes. Cover and cook over low heat until almost done.

Remove the meat from the oven, wrap in aluminum foil and let rest for around 15 minutes.

Increase the oven temperature to 225°C (425°F). Pour off 5 dl (2 cups) cooking liquid for sauce. Transfer the vegetables to the roasting tray and bake for around 15 minutes, while the meat is resting and while the sauce is being prepared. Heat the cooking liquid to boiling, stir the cornstarch into the water and whisk into the stock. Cook until thickened. Correct the seasoning. Serve the lamb with the baked vegetables, potatoes and au jus.

Roast lamb

Reindeer roast
6 servings

1 ½ kg (3 lb) boneless reindeer roast, rolled and tied
1 ½ teaspoons salt
1 ½ teaspoons pepper
2 carrots
1 onion
8 dl (3 ⅓ cups) water

Game sauce:
4 tablespoons (60 g/2 oz) butter
4 tablespoons (¼ cup) flour
8 dl (3 ⅓ cups) cooking liquid
2-3 juniper berries, crushed
1 dl (½ cup) sour heavy cream
2-3 slices brown goat cheese (Ski Queen)
or 1 tablespoon crushed lingonberries
½ teaspoon salt
½ teaspoon pepper

Preheat the oven to 175°C (350°F). Rub the meat with salt and pepper. Insert a meat thermometer into the thickest part. Place the meat in an oven tray. Cut the carrots into thick slices and the

onion into wedges and add. Pour over the water. Roast for around 1 ½ hours. When the internal temperature is 65°C (150°F), the meat is pink inside, when 70°C (160°F), it is gray. Let the meat rest while you prepare the sauce. Melt the butter in a saucepan and stir in the flour. Cook until golden. Strain the cooking juices and add gradually, whisking constantly. Heat to boiling, lower the heat and simmer for around 10 minutes. Add the juniper, sour cream, cheese or berries. Reheat to boiling and season with salt and pepper. Serve the roast with boiled potatoes, broccoli or Brussels sprouts, sautéed mushrooms and sauce.

Helpful hints
Poached pear halves filled with currant jelly are a good accompaniment to this dish.

This recipe is also suitable for moose or deer.

Pork steaks *with orange jus*
4 servings

2 tablespoons butter
4 pork steaks (around 140 g (5 oz) each
1 teaspoon salt
½ teaspoon pepper
1 teaspoon dried rosemary or 2 tablespoons fresh
juice of 2 oranges

16 clusters tagliatelle
1 teaspoon oil
2 carrots
1 leek

Brown the butter in a heavy pan and fry the meat quickly on both sides over relatively high heat. Sprinkle with salt, pepper and rosemary. Then add the orange juice. Cover, remove the pan from the heat, and let the meat rest for around

Pork steaks with orange jus

10 minutes. Clean the vegetables. Cut the carrots lengthwise into thin slices with a cheese plane. Cut the leek into thin rings. Cook the pasta in water with oil to prevent sticking. Add the carrot and leek around 3-4 minutes before the end of the cooking time. Serve the pork steaks with pasta and vegetables. Pour over the orange flavored juices and serve with homemade bread and a salad.

Steaks with mushroom-cream sauce

Steaks *with mushroom-cream sauce*
4 servings

4 thick steaks (sirloin, rib eye, strip loin and tenderloin), around 180 g (6 oz) each
1 teaspoon salt
1 teaspoon pepper
2 tablespoons butter

Mushroom-cream sauce
250 g (9 oz) fresh mushrooms
2 tablespoons butter
1/2 teaspoon salt
1/2 teaspoon pepper
2 dl (1 cup) stock or bouillon
2 dl (1 cup) whipping cream
1 teaspoon soy sauce
2 tablespoons chopped chives

Sprinkle the steaks with salt and pepper and sauté in butter over medium heat until drops of juice appear on the top. Turn and cook until new drops of juice appear. Then the meat is medium. Prepare the sauce: Clean and slice the mushrooms. Brown butter in a pan and add the mushrooms. Cook until golden. Sprinkle with salt and pepper. Add stock and cream and heat to boiling.

Let the sauce simmer for around 10 minutes, until somewhat thickened. Season to taste with soy sauce. Just before serving, sprinkle with chives. Serve with boiled potatoes.

Ham and mushroom sauce
for pasta
4 servings

250 g (8 oz) cooked ham
150 g (5 oz) fresh mushrooms
1 tablespoon butter
2 dl (1 cup) vegetable stock
2 dl (1 cup) whipping cream
2 tablespoons minced parsley
1/2 teaspoons lemon juice
1/2 teaspoon salt
1/2 teaspoon pepper
pasta
grated parmesan cheese

Cut the ham into strips. Slice the mushrooms and sauté in butter until golden. Add stock and cream and reduce the mixture over high heat. When thickened, stir in the ham and parsley. Season with lemon juice, salt and pepper. Serve over pasta and sprinkle with parmesan cheese.

Fried ham sandwich
4 servings

1-2 garlic cloves
1 tablespoon olive oil
8 slices white bread
12 slices boiled ham
1 avocado, in thin wedges
8 lettuce leaves
1-2 tomatoes, sliced
1 teaspoon lemon juice

Pasta with ham and mushroom sauce

½ teaspoon coarsely ground pepper

Mince the garlic and sauté in olive oil. Add the bread and fry on both sides. Remove from the pan. Sauté the ham and avocado. Arrange lettuce and tomato on 4 slices of the bread. Top with ham and avocado. Season with lemon juice and pepper. Top with the remaining bread. Halve on the diagonal. Eat while warm!

Helpful hint
Use different kinds of meat. Try shredded pork. Sauté it in oil for 2-3 minutes.

Fried ham sandwich

Reindeer strips
with mushroom and cheese sauce
4 servings

500 g (1 ¼ lb) shaved reindeer
1-2 tablespoons butter
1 teaspoon salt
½ teaspoon pepper
150 g (5 oz) fresh mushrooms
200 g (7 oz) bacon-flavored cheese spread
2 dl (1 cup) game or beef stock
1 tablespoon chopped fresh thyme or rosemary
or 1 teaspoon dried

Defrost the meat slightly. Sauté in a hot pan with
a little butter. Season with salt and pepper. Do
not use too much salt, as the cheese is salty.
Quarter the mushrooms and add. Sauté lightly
with the meat. Add the cheese and stock and stir
until the cheese has melted. Cook over medium
heat until well mixed. Sprinkle with herbs. Serve
with boiled potatoes, Brussels sprouts and lingonberry compote.

Helpful hint
This dish tastes even better when topped with
crispy bacon slices.

Any kind of game is also good in this dish, and
you can shave it yourself. Defrost the meat slightly, then cut paper thin slices with a sharp knife.
Fry in a hot pan.

Pork chops *with braised vegetables*
4 servings

4 pork chops
2 tablespoons oil
3 garlic cloves
1 teaspoon salt
½ teaspoon coarsely ground pepper
2 bell peppers, red and/or yellow
1 zucchini
1 dried pepper or 1 chili
3 tablespoons olives
1 ½ dl (⅔ cup) white wine or cider

Sauté the chops in oil for 2 minutes per side over
medium heat. Sprinkle with salt and pepper.
Remove from the pan and keep warm. Cut the
vegetables into strips and chop the chili. Sauté
quickly in the same pan and add the wine. Top
with the chops, cover and let simmer over low
heat for around 10 minutes. Serve with bread,
rice or boiled potatoes.

Reindeer strips with mushroom and cheese sauce

95

Lamb chops *with pizzaiola sauce*

8 lamb chops
olive oil
1 teaspoon salt
½ teaspoon pepper
2 tablespoons shredded fresh basil or 1 teaspoon
dried

Pizzaiola sauce

1 onion
2 garlic cloves
1 can (14 oz) chopped tomatoes
2 tablespoons tomato paste
1 dl (⅓ cup) pitted black olives

Brown the chops in oil in a hot cast iron pan for
around 1 minute per side. Sprinkle with salt, pepper and basil. Lower the heat and continue cooking for 3-4 minutes. Clean and mince the onion
and garlic. Sauté in oil until shiny, add the tomatoes and tomato paste, and reduce slightly. Just
before serving, halve the olives and add. Serve
the chops with the sauce, pasta, lemon wedges
and crusty bread.

Smoked pork loin
with creamed vegetables
4 servings

1 – 1 ½ kg (2 ¼ - 3 lb) smoked pork loin
1 teaspoon freshly ground pepper

Creamed vegetables

3 carrots
3 rutabaga slices
½ celeriac
2 dl (1 cup) water
½ teaspoon salt
1 tablespoon flour
1-2 dl (½ – 1 cup) milk
2 tablespoons butter
ground nutmeg

Preheat the oven to 175°C (350°F). Place the
meat in an ovenproof dish and sprinkle with pepper. Insert a meat thermometer into the thickest
part. Roast for 1 – 1 ½ hours, until the internal
temperature reaches 72°C (165°F). Let the meat
rest for at least 15 minutes before carving into slices. While the meat is cooking, prepare the vegetables. Clean and cut the vegetables into 2 cm
(¾") cubes. Cook in the water (it should just
cover the vegetables) with a little salt until tender.
Place flour and milk in a jar and shake until blended. Pour in a thin stream over the vegetables,
stirring well. Heat to boiling, add the butter and
cook for 3-4 minutes. Season with a little nutmeg. Serve with boiled potatoes.

Roast ribs of pork

4 servings

2 kg (4 ½ lb) pork belly, with bones and rind
2-3 teaspoons salt
1 teaspoon pepper

Count on 500 g (1 lb) per person.

Score the rind

Cut through the rind and slightly into the fat with a sharp pointed knife. If you score the rind parallel with the bones, it will be easier to slice after roasting. If the ribs are frozen, it's a good idea to score the rind when still partially frozen, as that makes the task easier.

Seasoning

Rub the ribs with salt and pepper 1-3 days before roasting, being sure to get salt into every part of the roast. Place the ribs in an oven tray, rind down and cover with aluminum foil. Refrigerate until ready to roast. This gives the seasonings time to penetrate the meat.

Roasting

Turn the ribs rind side up. Place an upside down dish under the ribs to raise them slightly in the middle (that way, the melted fat runs off). For even roasting, the ribs should be the same thickness on both sides. Pour over 2 dl (1 cup) water and cover the pan with aluminum foil. Preheat the oven to 230°C (450°F). Roast the foil-covered ribs on the center shelf for around 45 minutes. The ribs should "blow up" a little and the rind should crack. Remove the foil (but leave the dish) and lower the oven temperature to 200°C (400°F). Continue roasting for around 1½ hours. Sometimes the rind becomes crispy on its own. If this doesn't happen, move the pan to the top oven shelf and increase the temperature to 250°C (475°), or turn on the grill. Do not burn the rind.

If parts of the rind are already crispy, cover them with foil. When all the rind is crisp, remove the meat from the oven and let it rest for at least 15 minutes before carving. The traditional Norwegian Christmas accompaniments, such as pork patties, pork sausages, apples and prunes, can be roasted in the pan with the ribs for the final 20 minutes of cooking time.

Serve the ribs with natural juices or brown gravy, sauerkraut or pickled red cabbage – and prunes, apples, lefse and lingonberry compote.

Helpful Hint
To avoid a mad rush before everyone comes for dinner, you can prepare the ribs earlier in the day. Let the ribs rest for a while before cutting into serving pieces. Place in an oven tray along with pork patties and sausages and reheat at 200°C (400°F) for 30 minutes.

Gravy
1 packet brown gravy mix
chopped fried shallots
rose and green peppercorns

For added flavor, use a packet of gravy mix to thicken the natural pan juices. Prepare according to package directions, but use pan juices (be sure to skim off the fat first) instead of water. Add shallots and peppercorns, if desired.

See recipe for pork patties on page 112.

Roast dried ribs of mutton
4 servings

Count on 350 g (11 oz) mutton ribs per person

If you have a whole side of ribs, it's a good idea to cut between each rib for chops. Soak the ribs in cold water overnight. Change water several times. Place a metal rack or birch twigs (without bark) in the bottom of a large pot. Fill with water to the edge of the rack. Arrange the meat on the rack. Cover and simmer until the meat practically falls off the bones, around 2 hours. Check frequently – do not let the pan cook dry. For more color, the pinnekjøtt can be browned lightly in the oven. Arrange in an oven tray and place on the top shelf under the grill for around 5 minutes. If serving sausages alongside, steam them with the meat for the last 15-20 minutes. Serve pinnekjøtt on heated plates with coarsely ground sausages, mashed rutabagas, pan juices from the meat, boiled potatoes and mustard.

Mashed rutabagas, see page 117.

Soak the tomatoes and mushrooms in water for around 2 hours. Brown the meat on both sides in oil in a heavy pan. Coarsely chop the vegetables, including the tomatoes and mushrooms, and add. Sauté for 3-4 minutes. Add the wine and cover. Lower the heat and let simmer for around 1 ½ hours. Sprinkle with parsley just before serving. Serve with hearty bread.

Seamen's stew

4 servings

600 g boneless beef stew meat
butter
3-4 dl (1 ¼-1 ½ cups) water or stock
6 potatoes
2-3 carrots
1 thick slice rutabaga
1 parsley root

Cube the meat and brown on all sides in butter in small batches. Transfer to a pot and add the water or stock. Peel and cube the vegetables and add. Simmer over medium heat until meat and vegetables are tender, around 1 hour. Stir as little as possible to avoid breaking down the vegetables, but make sure that nothing burns. Season with salt and pepper. Serve with whole grain bread or flatbread and lingonberry compote.

If you are in a hurry, you don't have to brown the meat. You can also use leftover meat in this dish.

Osso bucco

4-6 servings

150 g (5 oz) sun-dried tomatoes
100 g (3 ½ oz) dried mushrooms (such as porcini or chanterelles)
6 slices veal shank on the bone
3 tablespoons olive oil
2 onions
1 celeriac
2 carrots
3 cups dry white wine
1 teaspoon salt
1 teaspoon coarsely ground pepper
2 tablespoons chopped fresh parsley

Seaman's stew

Boiled beef and soup

with onion sauce
4 servings

1 ¼ liters (6 cups) water
1 ¼ kg (2 ½ lb) chuck, arm, brisket or short ribs, with bone
1 teaspoon salt
1 small leek
3 carrots
100 g (4 oz) celeriac or parsley root
150 g (5 oz) cabbage
½ teaspoon pepper

Onion sauce
1 onion, finely chopped
5 dl (2 cups) beef stock
2 tablespoons flour
½ dl (¼ cup) cold water
2 teaspoons 7% vinegar
1 tablespoon sugar

Heat the water to boiling and add the meat, keeping the pieces as whole as possible. Reheat to boiling, skimming well. Add salt and the green part of the leek. Cover and let simmer until the meat is tender, about 1½ hours. Skim off any fat with a slotted spoon. Slice the remaining leek. Peel and cube the carrots and celeriac. Shred the cabbage. Add to the pot and simmer until tender, around 10 minutes. While the vegetables are cooking, remove around 5 dl (2 cups) cooking liquid for the onion sauce. In a saucepan, heat the cooking liquid and onion to boiling. Place flour and water in a small jar and shake. Whisk into the stock. Heat to boiling, lower the heat and let simmer for around 10 minutes. Season with vinegar, sugar, salt and pepper. Serve the soup first. Slice the meat and serve with boiled potatoes, soup vegetables and onion sauce.

Lamb fricassee

4 servings

1 kg (2 ¼ lb) lamb shoulder on the bone
6 dl (2 ½ cups) water
2 carrots
2 parsley roots
1 cauliflower
1 leek
6 dl (2 ½ cups) stock
4 tablespoons (¼ cup) flour dissolved in a little cold water
3 tablespoons fresh dill or 1 tablespoon dried
2 ½ tablespoons sour cream
1 tablespoon lemon juice

Boiled beef and soup

Lamb fricassee

Cut the meat into serving pieces. Heat the water to boiling, then add the meat. Reheat to boiling, skimming well. Add the salt and let the meat simmer for around 45 minutes. Clean and cut the vegetables into chunks and add. Simmer for around 10 minutes, until the vegetables are tender. Prepare the sauce in the same pot or use a new saucepan. Heat the cooking liquid to boiling, whisk in the flour mixture. Simmer for around 10 minutes. Add the remaining ingredients, seasoning with a little salt and pepper, if necessary. Serve with boiled potatoes.

Lamb and cabbage stew

Lightly salted ham hocks

Lamb and cabbage stew

4 servings

1 ¹/₂ kg (3 lb) cabbage
1 ¹/₂ kg (3 lb) mutton or lamb shoulder on the bone, in chunks
2 teaspoons salt
4 teaspoons black peppercorns
3 dl (1 ¹/₄ cups) water

Cut the cabbage into wedges. Layer the meat and cabbage in a pot, sprinkling salt and pepper between the layers. The peppercorns can be

placed in a tea-ball, if desired. Add the water. Heat to boiling, cover, then lower the heat and simmer over low heat until the meat is tender, 1 ¹/₂ - 2 hours. Serve piping hot on heated plates with boiled potatoes. For thicker pan juices, sprinkle 1-2 tablespoons flour between the layers of meat and cabbage.

Lightly salted ham hocks
4-6 servings

2 ³/₄ liter (11 cups) water, or enough to cover the meat
4 lightly salted and smoked ham hocks

Heat the water to boiling and add the hocks. Do not add salt. The meat should be completely submerged. Lower the heat, cover and cook at a slow simmer for around 3 hours. Serve with boiled potatoes and dumplings (page 27).

Innherred soup

This is a festive dish, traditionally served at christenings, confirmations and weddings in rural Norway.

8 servings

Stock

2 ¹/₂ kg (5 lb) mutton and beef on the bone
3 ¹/₂ liters (14 cups) water
2 ¹/₂ tablespoons salt
1 teaspoon ground ginger
1 teaspoon peppercorns
1 onion

Meatballs

400 g (14 oz) boneless mutton and beef

100 g (3 ½ oz) suet

1 ½ teaspoons salt

½ teaspoon white pepper

1 teaspoon flour

2 teaspoons potato starch

1 teaspoon grated onion

2 dl (¾ cup) light cream

Begin with the stock. Remove the meat from the bones and cut into cubes. Reserve 400 g (14 oz) for the meatballs. Cut the bones into smaller chunks and place in a pot with the water. Heat to boiling, skimming well. Add the salt, pepper and ginger. Quarter the onion and add. Lower the heat, cover and let simmer for at least 2 hours. Strain. Simmer the meat in the stock until tender, 30-45 minutes. For the meatballs, grind the meat and suet with salt 3-4 times. For an extra fine texture, use a food processor. Add the flour, pepper and onion, and with the motor running, add the cream in a thin stream. Make small meatballs and poach in a little of the stock. Just before serving, reheat the meatballs in the soup. Serve with boiled potatoes, carrots and leeks and flatbread.

Innherred soup

Grandmother's pea soup

4 servings

200 g (8 oz) dried yellow peas
1 onion
1 celeriac slice
1 dried ham hock or bones from a leg of mutton
2 liters (8 ¼ cups) water
1 teaspoon dried thyme or 1 tablespoon chopped fresh
2 carrots
1 leek

Soak the peas in water overnight. Drain and return the peas to the pot. Coarsely chop the onion and celeriac and add with the meat. Add the water and thyme and heat to boiling. Lower the heat and let simmer for 2-3 hours. Around 20 minutes before the soup is ready, slice the carrot and leek and add. Remove the hock, cut off the meat, cut into bite-size pieces and return to the soup. Serve with potatoes and flatbread.

Helpful hint:
This soup can be made with all kinds of salted meat. Chose a cut on the bone for more flavor.

Meat soup

4 servings

800 g (1 ¾ lb) boneless front-quarter meat
1 liter (4 cups) stock
½ teaspoon dried thyme
1 onion
1 rutabaga
1 celeriac
1 leek
4 potatoes
½ teaspoon salt and pepper
Cut the meat into 3 cm (1 ¼") cubes. Cook in stock with thyme until tender, around 40 minutes. Clean and cut the vegetables into large chunks and add during the last 15 minutes of cooking time. Season with salt, pepper and more thyme, if desired. Serve with crusty bread or rolls.

Helpful hint
This soup is excellent when made with moose or reindeer.

Grandmothers peasoup

Meat soup

Bolognese sauce

4 servings

1 onion
2 celery stalks
1 carrot
3 bacon slices
500 g (1 ¼ lb) ground beef
2 tablespoons tomato paste

1 can (14 oz) tomatoes
3 dl (1 ¼ cups) stock
½-1 teaspoon salt
½ teaspoon pepper
1 teaspoon dried oregano

Clean and chop the vegetables. Cut the bacon into shreds. Brown the ground beef without added fat over medium heat. Add the vegetables, bacon, tomato paste, tomatoes and stock. Let simmer for around 20 minutes. Add the seasonings. Serve over spaghetti and top with grated Parmesan cheese. Serve with a salad and garlic bread.

Helpful hint:
This sauce is also good on pizza. Cook it a little longer, so that more liquid evaporates and the filling is thicker.

over medium heat for about 5 minutes per side. Transfer to a pot and simmer in stock or water for around 10 minutes.

Strain the pan juices for gravy, add the onion and heat to boiling. Whisk in the flour mixture and heat to boiling, stirring constantly. Let simmer for 7-8 minutes, then season with salt and pepper. Serve with boiled potatoes and lingonberry compote.

Meat patties *with brown gravy*
4 servings

500 g (1 ½ lb) ground beef
1 ½ teaspoons salt
¼ teaspoon pepper
¼ teaspoon nutmeg
¼ teaspoon ground ginger
2 ½ tablespoons potato starch
2 dl (¾ cup) water or milk
butter

Brown gravy
5 dl (2 cups) stock or cooking juices
1 onion, minced
3 tablespoons flour stirred into a small amount of cold water
salt, pepper
soy sauce

Mix the ground meat with salt until elastic. Stir in the seasonings and starch, mixing thoroughly. Gradually add the liquid, mixing it thoroughly into the meat before adding more. Form the meat mixture into round patties. Fry in butter

Lasagna
4 servings

Meat sauce:

1 onion
1 carrot
100 g (4 oz) mushrooms
500 g (1 ¼ lb) ground beef
½-1 teaspoon salt
½ teaspoon pepper
2 tablespoons tomato paste
3 dl (1 ¼ cups) beef stock
1 can (14 oz) chopped tomatoes

Clean and chop the vegetables. Brown the meat in a dry pan. Sprinkle with salt and pepper. Add vegetables, tomato paste, stock and tomatoes. Let simmer for around 20 minutes.

Cheese sauce:

1 tablespoon butter
2 tablespoons flour
4 dl (1 ⅔ cups) milk
1 dl (½ cup) grated mozzarella or Swiss cheese
1 teaspoon salt
½ teaspoon white pepper
¼ teaspoon nutmeg

Melt the butter and stir in the flour. Gradually whisk in the milk. Let simmer for around 10 minutes. The sauce should be rather thick. Stir in the cheese. Season with salt, pepper and nutmeg.

9 pre-cooked lasagna noodles
1-2 dl (½-1 cup) grated cheese

Preheat the oven to 225°C (450°F). Layer the lasagna noodles, meat sauce and cheese sauce in a greased pan, beginning with noodles and ending with cheese sauce. Top with grated cheese. Bake for 30-40 minutes. Let the lasagna

rest for around 10 minutes before serving. Serve with Italian bread and a salad.

Moussaka
4 servings

2-3 eggplants
1 ½ teaspoons salt
2 tablespoons olive oil
2 onions
2 garlic cloves
1 bunch parsley
400 g (14 oz) ground lamb
2 dl (1 cup) stock
1 can (14 oz) chopped tomatoes
½ teaspoon dried thyme
½ teaspoon dried rosemary
½ teaspoon ground cinnamon

Bechamel sauce

2 tablespoons butter

3 tablespoons flour

4 dl (1 2/3 cups) milk

$\frac{1}{2}$ teaspoon salt

$\frac{1}{4}$ teaspoon white pepper

2 eggs

1 dl (1/2 cup) grated mozzarella or Swiss cheese

Cut the eggplants into $\frac{1}{2}$ cm ($\frac{3}{16}$") slices. Place on paper towels and sprinkle with salt on both sides. Let marinate for 1 hour, then rinse under cold water. Dry well. Brown lightly on both sides in oil. Drain on paper towels. Mince the onion, garlic and parsley and brown lightly. Add the meat and fry until golden. Add the stock, tomatoes with juice and seasonings. Let simmer over low heat for 25-40 minutes. Add more liquid if necessary. Preheat the oven to 225°C (450°F). For the béchamel sauce, melt the butter and stir in the flour. Whisk in the milk and add the seasonings. Cook until thickened. Whisk in the eggs. Layer the eggplant, meat sauce, béchamel sauce and grated cheese in a greased ovenproof dish, ending with cheese. Bake for around 30 minutes. Serve with crusty bread and a salad.

Moussaka

Pork patties

6 servings

1 kg (2 ¼ lb) ground pork
1 tablespoon salt
2 cups milk
5 tablespoons (1/3 cup) potato starch
¾ teaspoon ground pepper
½ teaspoon ground nutmeg
¼ teaspoon ground ginger
oil

Brown gravy
4 tablespoons (¼ cup) butter
4 tablespoons (¼ cup) flour
8 dl (3 ⅓ cups) hot stock
1 teaspoon soy sauce
salt, pepper

Mix the pork thoroughly with the salt. Gradually stir in ⅔ of the milk. Start slowly, increasing gradually. Mix thoroughly. The mixture should become quite elastic with each addition of liquid. Add the starch and seasonings, then the remaining milk. Make round patties and brown in oil on both sides. Add a little water or stock and simmer until cooked through, 4-5 minutes. Use the cooking juices to make gravy. Melt the butter and let it turn golden brown. Add the flour and cook until nut brown. Gradually whisk in the stock. Let simmer uncovered for around 10 minutes. Add the soy sauce. Season with salt and pepper if necessary. Serve with mashed potatoes and cooked vegetables.

Sausage omelet
4 servings

2 smoked sausages
1 small red bell pepper
4 mushrooms
2 tablespoons butter
8 eggs
1 dl (⅓ cup) water
1 ½ teaspoons salt
2 tablespoons chopped chives

Cube the sausages and pepper. Slice the mushrooms. Fry in butter. Remove from the pan and set aside. Beat the eggs with water and salt and pour the mixture into the pan. Cook until the omelet is set in the center. Arrange the filling on one side of the omelet and fold the other half over. Sprinkle with chives. Serve with a salad and bread.

Helpful hint
Other kinds of sausages, including dried ones can be used in this dish.

Sausage omelet

Curried sausage *with apples*
4 servings

2 apples
1 onion
2 tablespoons butter
2 teaspoons curry powder
600 g (1 ⅓ lb) sausages (frankfurters or bratwurst)

Cube the apple and cut the onion into wedges. Fry in butter, then sprinkle with curry powder. Keep warm. Fry the sausages. Serve with mash potatoes and garnish with fresh herbs.

Curried sausage with apples

Side dishes

Baked potatoes
4 servings

4 large potatoes
salt

Preheat the oven to 200°C (400°F). Wash the potatoes well. Cut an x in each potato. Place in an ovenproof dish. Bake until soft all the way through, from 60 to 80 minutes. Remove the potatoes from the oven and let rest for a few minutes. Break open at the x, or cut through. Spoon on desired filling.

Filling:
– Sour cream and crisp bacon bits
– Sour cream and shrimp, crab or lobster
– Herb butter
– Mushroom sauce
– Pickled herring, beets, onion and sour cream
– Bacon, tomato, cucumber and sour cream
– Grated cheese
– Blue cheese blended with butter

Garlic butter
3 tablespoons butter
2 garlic cloves
chopped parsley and/or chives

Beat the butter until soft. Mince the garlic and add with the parsley. Place on plastic wrap and form into a roll. Freeze until solid. Slice and serve with baked potatoes. Garnish with parsley.

Mushroom sauce
50 g (2 oz) fresh mushrooms
1 teaspoon lemon juice
2 dl (1 cup) sour cream
3 tablespoons minced parsley
1 tablespoon minced oregano
salt and pepper

Finely chop the mushrooms and combine with the remaining ingredients, seasoning with salt and pepper to taste.

If you can't get fresh oregano, use 1 teaspoon dried.

Scalloped potatoes
4 servings

8 potatoes
2 garlic cloves
1 teaspoon salt
$1/2$ teaspoon pepper
2 $1/2$ dl (1 cup) whipping cream
grated cheese

Preheat the oven to 200°C (400°F). Peel and slice the potatoes. Peel and mince the garlic. Arrange in a greased ovenproof dish. Sprinkle with salt and pepper. Pour cream over potatoes. Bake for 20 minutes. Remove from the oven and sprinkle with cheese. Bake for around 40 minutes, until potatoes are tender.

You can also add minced onion, leek or bell pepper. Half and half or even milk can be used instead of cream. Cooking time is lowered if the potatoes are parboiled in cream/milk for a few minutes.

Baked potato wedges

Preheat the oven to 200°C (400°F). Wash and dry the potatoes well. Cut into wedges and arrange on an oven tray. Drizzle with oil, tossing to coat. Sprinkle with ground paprika, salt, pepper and your choice of herbs. Bake until potatoes are tender, around 30 minutes.

Rösti

Count on 200 g (8 oz) potato per person. Peel, wash and coarsely shred the potatoes. Press out the water. Heat oil in a skillet and spread a handful of potato over the pan. Fry until golden brown on one side. Ease the potato cake onto a lid to simplify turning onto the other side and fry until golden. Season just before serving. Excellent with both fried meat and fish.

You can sprinkle rösti with grated cheese and serve it on its own with bacon.

Potatoes boulangère

4 servings

1 kilo (2 ¼ lb) potatoes
200 g (8 oz) onion
oil
salt and pepper
5 dl (2 cups) stock

Preheat the oven to 200°C (400°F). Peel and slice the potatoes and onion. Sauté quickly in oil and sprinkle with salt and pepper. Transfer to an ovenproof dish. Pour the stock over the potatoes. Cover and bake for 10 minutes. Turn the potatoes and bake until tender, around 15 minutes.

From left: Baked potato wedges, potatoes boulangère and rösti

Potato puree
Use 2 medium potatoes per serving

4 servings

1 kg (2 ¼ lb) potatoes
2 dl milk
100 g (3 ½ oz) butter
salt and white pepper
grated nutmeg

Peel and cook the potatoes in unsalted water
until tender. Drain and mash. Stir in milk and
butter. Reheat and season with salt, pepper and
nutmeg.

Norwegian ratatouille
4 servings

6 tomatoes
300 g (10 oz) zucchini
1 red bell pepper
1 green bell pepper
2-3 onions
2 garlic cloves
oil
2 tablespoons tomato paste
salt and pepper
minced parsley

Peel and dice the tomatoes. Dice the zucchini and
peppers. Mince the onion and garlic. Sauté onion
and garlic in oil until shiny. Add remaining vegetables and tomato paste. Simmer until tender.
Season with salt and pepper and sprinkle with
parsley.

Norwegian ratatouille

Mashed rutabagas
4 servings

1 kg (2 ¼ lb) rutabaga
1 liter (4 cups) water
½ teaspoon pepper
2 teaspoons salt
½ dl (¼ cup) stock

Peel and slice the rutabaga. Cook until tender in
lightly salted water. Drain, then mash. Season
with pepper, salt and stock from the pinnekjøtt.

Carrot cream

4 servings

¹/₂ teaspoon dried dill
¹/₂ teaspoon dried basil
2 teaspoons chopped parsley
1 teaspoon chopped chives
3 dl (1 ¹/₄ cups) cottage cheese
3 dl (1 ¹/₄ cups) grated carrot

Stir seasonings into cottage cheese. Fold in the carrots.

Delicious with bread or as a side dish with fish or meat. Store covered in the refrigerator.

Stewed peas

4 servings

500 g (1 lb) dried green peas
60 g (2 oz) butter
1 tablespoon salt
1 teaspoon sugar
white pepper

Rinse peas and soak in cold water overnight. Let simmer in soaking water until tender. If too much water, drain off any excess. Add salt, sugar, pepper and butter. Good with *lutefisk* and meat cakes.

Creamed cabbage

750 g (1 ²/₃ lb) cabbage
2 tablespoons butter
4 tablespoons (1/4 cup) flour
4 dl (1 ²/₃ cups) milk (or 3 parts milk and 1 part cabbage water)
¹/₂ teaspoon salt
pinch grated nutmeg

Shred the cabbage and cook in lightly salted water until tender. Drain the cabbage, reserving 1 dl (1/2 cup) of the cooking liquid. Melt the butter and stir in the flour. Gradually whisk in the milk (or milk and cabbage water). Heat to boiling, stirring constantly. Let simmer for around 5 minutes, then season with salt and nutmeg. Stir the cabbage into the sauce and reheat to boiling.

Mashed roots

4 servings

4 carrots, in chunks
1 potato, in chunks
3 slices rutabaga, in chunks
2-3 tablespoons milk or light cream

2 tablespoons butter
salt, pepper, grated nutmeg, minced parsley

Cook the vegetables until tender. Reserve the cooking liquid. Mash the vegetables, adding cooking liquid and milk to desired thickness. Stir in the butter and season with salt, pepper and nutmeg. Garnish with parsley

Norwegian sauerkraut

4 servings

1 ¹/₄ kg (2 ¹/₂ lb) cabbage, finely shredded
2 apples, peeled, cored and thinly sliced
125 g (4 oz) butter
1 ¹/₂ teaspoons salt
125 g (²/₃ cup) sugar
1 teaspoon caraway seed
2 dl (1 cup) water
1 dl (¹/₂ cup) 7% vinegar

Layer cabbage and apple slices in a pot with butter, sprinkling each layer with seasonings. Add water and let simmer for around 1 hour. Add vinegar to taste, adding more sugar and salt as necessary. Good with roast pork ribs and meat cakes.

Tomato salad

4 servings

lettuce
6 tomatoes
1 onion
1 dl (½ cup) fresh bean sprouts
fresh basil

Dressing
4 tablespoons (¼ cup) olive oil
1 tablespoon red wine vinegar
1 tablespoon fresh lemon juice
1 teaspoon prepared mustard
salt and pepper

Arrange lettuce leaves in a bowl. Thinly slice tomatoes and onion and layer in the bowl with sprouts and basil. Mix dressing and pour over salad.

Add 1 minced garlic clove to dressing, if desired.

Waldorf salad

Waldorf salad

4 servings

100 g (4 oz) cabbage
100 g (4 oz) grapes
2 apples
2 pineapple rings
2 celery stalks
1 dl (½ cup) chopped walnuts

Dressing
1 dl (½ cup) whipping cream
1 dl (½ cup) mayonnaise
1½ teaspoons fresh lemon juice
2 teaspoons sugar

Shred the cabbage. Halve the grapes, removing any seeds. Dice the apples and pineapple. Thinly slice the celery. Combine with nuts. Whip the cream. Fold in the mayonnaise, lemon juice and sugar. Pour over the salad, mixing gently to combine. Serve on a platter garnished with grapes, pineapple chunks and chopped nuts.

Waldorf salad is excellent with turkey and chicken, baked ham, tongue and roast beef, and it can be made ahead of time.

Blue dot salad

4 servings

1 leaf lettuce
½ seedless cucumber
2 celery stalks
1 grapefruit
10 blue grapes

Dressing
2 tablespoons sour cream
4 tablespoons (¼ cup) cottage cheese

Shred the lettuce and arrange in a bowl. Cut the cucumber into chunks. Thinly slice the celery. Peel and divide the grapefruit into sections. Halve each section. Halve the grapes. Mix the dressing. Layer ingredients (except for the grapes) and dressing in the bowl. Top with the grapes.

This salad is good with meat and fish.

Salad dressings

Sour cream dressing

2 dl (1 cup) sour cream
prepared mustard
lemon juice
salt and pepper

Mix ingredients together.

Garlic dressing

1 garlic clove
2 tablespoons wine vinegar
salt and freshly ground pepper
4 tablespoons (¼ cup) olive oil

Mince garlic and combine with vinegar, salt and pepper. Whisk in oil until emulsified.

Mustard dressing

This recipe uses raw egg yolk. Use only safety-checked eggs.

1 egg yolk
1 tablespoon Dijon mustard
1 tablespoon wine vinegar
salt and pepper
4 tablespoons (¼ cup) olive oil

Whisk egg yolk with mustard, vinegar, salt and pepper. Whisk in oil until emulsified.

Mild sour cream dressing

2 dl (1 cup) sour cream
2 tablespoons mayonnaise
1 tablespoon fresh lemon juice
1 tablespoon chopped scallions or chives
salt and white pepper

Combine sour cream and mayonnaise. Whisk in remaining ingredients, seasoning to taste with salt and pepper.

Low-fat sour cream and mayonnaise can be used in this dressing.

Blue cheese dressing

2 dl (1 cup) sour cream
1 tablespoon fresh lemon juice
75 g (2 ½ oz) blue cheese
2 tablespoons chopped chives

Stir sour cream and lemon juice together. Crumble cheese and add. Fold in chives.

Spring dressing

6 tablespoons olive oil
2 tablespoons fresh lemon juice
1 garlic clove, minced
salt and freshly ground pepper
Combine all ingredients in a jar and shake well.

Vinaigrette

2-3 tablespoons olive oil
1 tablespoon wine vinegar or fresh lemon juice
¼ teaspoon salt
⅛ teaspoon white pepper

Combine all ingredients in a jar and shake well.

The usual proportions in vinaigrette are 3 table-spoons oil to 1 tablespoon vinegar. For less oily flavor, reduce the amount of oil to 2 tablespoons. Store all dressings in the refrigerator.

Desserts

Red dessert

4-6 servings

3 dl (1 ¼ cups) red berry juice (if using concentrate, dilute to drink strength)
3 dl (1 ¼ cups) water
around 60 g (3 tablespoons) semolina
1 tablespoon sugar

Heat the juice and water to boiling. Whisk in the
semolina. Let simmer over low heat for around
15 minutes. Whisk in the sugar. Transfer to a
bowl and let cool completely. Serve with vanilla
sauce (see page 133).

Rhubarb soup

4-6 servings

1 liter (4 cups) water
300 g (1 ¼ cups) sugar
1 vanilla bean
500 g (1 lb) rhubarb
1 tablespoon finely shredded mint
sliced strawberries
vanilla ice cream

Heat water and sugar to boiling. Split the vanilla
bean lengthwise and scrape out the seeds. Add
bean and seeds to sugar syrup and let simmer for
around 15 minutes.

Wash, peel and cut the rhubarb into chunks. Add
to the syrup with the mint and remove from the
heat. Cover and let steep until cold. Remove the
vanilla bean. Serve with strawberries and ice
cream. Garnish with mint leaves, if desired.

Rhubarb soup

Red dessert

Fruit salad

7-8 servings

3 oranges
3 kiwi fruit
200 g (8 oz) purple grapes
100 g (4 oz) chopped almonds
3 red apples
2 bananas
1 can (300g/11 oz) pineapple chunks packed in juice

Peel oranges and kiwi. Halve the grapes and remove the seeds. Toast the nuts in a dry pan until golden. Let cool. Cut apple, orange sections and kiwi into chunks. Peel the banana and cut into chunks. Combine all fruit with the pineapple and juice. Let marinate for at least two hours in the refrigerator before serving. Sprinkle with nuts and serve with raw cream or herbed vanilla sauce (see page 133).

Baked apples

4 servings

75 g (⅓ cup) butter
150 g (1 cup) flour
1-2 tablespoons water
4 medium apples
2 tablespoons ground almonds
2 tablespoons sugar
1 egg yolk
2 tablespoons currants
1 tablespoon confectioner's sugar
beaten egg white

Cut butter and flour together with a pastry blender. Add water and mix lightly together. Form into a ball and let rest for around 1 hour. Preheat the oven to 200°C (400°F). Peel and core the apples. Combine almonds, sugar, egg yolk, currants and confectioner's sugar and spoon into the holes in the apples. Roll the dough into a large sheet. Divide into 4 squares and place an apple on the center of each. Fold the dough over the apples, overlapping at the top. Glue together with egg white. Place in a greased baking dish (not too close together) with the seam down. Brush with the remaining egg white. Bake for around 20 minutes. Serve warm with vanilla sauce (page 133) or whipped cream.

Baked apples

Strawberry dessert

5-6 servings

1 liter (4 cups) strawberries
sugar
½ liter (1 pint) vanilla ice cream
1 liter (4 cups) strawberry yogurt

Clean the berries and mix with sugar. Layer berries, ice cream and yogurt in a bowl and stir carefully together.

Strawberry dessert

Veiled country lass

4 servings

5-6 apples
75 g (⅓ cup) sugar
2 dl (1 cup) water
3-4 dl (1 ½ cups) dry breadcrumbs
4 tablespoons (¼ cup) sugar
2 tablespoons butter
2-3 dl (1 cup) whipping cream

Peel and core the apples and cut into chunks.
Cook in sugar water until just tender. Let cool.
Combine bread, sugar and butter in a frying pan
and cook until golden and crisp. Let cool. Whip
the cream until light and fluffy. Layer the apple
compote, crumbs and cream in a glass bowl.
Garnish with chopped almonds, if desired.

Troll cream

4-6 servings

7 ½ dl (3 cups) lingonberries
1 ½ dl (½ cup) sugar
1 egg white
lingonberries

Combine all ingredients in a food processor and
process until thick and stiff. Transfer to a dessert
bowl and sprinkle with berries. Garnish with fresh
herbs, if desired. Serve with vanilla sauce and
crispy cone cookies.

Rice cream

4-6 servings

3 dl (1 ¼ cups) whipping cream
1 tablespoon sugar
1 teaspoon vanilla extract
3-4 dl (1 ½ cups) rice porridge
50 g (⅓ cup) chopped almonds

Whip the cream, sugar and vanilla until light and fluffy. Mix in the porridge and almonds. Serve with raspberry coulis or homemade red berry sauce.

Cloudberry cream

6 servings

5 dl (2 cups) whipping cream
1 teaspoon sugar
2 ½ dl (1 cup) lightly sweetened cloudberries

Whip the cream and sugar until light and fluffy. Carefully fold in the berries.

Rice cream

Palace dessert

4 servings

3 dl (1 ¼ cups) whipping cream
1 dl (½ cup) chocolate sauce
10-12 meringues
10-12 almonds, chopped and toasted until golden

Whip the cream until light and fluffy. Layer cream and meringues and drizzle with chocolate sauce. Sprinkle with nuts.

Semolina pudding

4 servings

1 liter (quart) milk
1 ¼ dl (½ cup) semolina
1 tablespoon sugar
1 egg
3 drops almond extract

Combine milk and semolina in a saucepan and heat to boiling, stirring constantly. Let simmer for around 15 minutes. Whisk sugar and egg in a bowl. Whisk in a little hot porridge, then whisk that mixture back into the saucepan of porridge. Reheat to boiling, stirring constantly. Add almond extract to taste. Transfer to a bowl and sprinkle with a little sugar. Let cool and serve with red berry sauce.

Heavenly dessert

This dessert contains raw eggs. Use only safely-checked eggs.

6 servings

5 gelatin sheets
2 eggs
1 dl (½ cup) sugar
1 dl (¼ cup) sherry or orange juice
3 tablespoons chopped almonds
3 tablespoons chopped candied cherries
2 tablespoons chopped chocolate
3 dl (1 ¼ cups) whipping cream

Soak the gelatin in cold water for around 5 minutes. Beat eggs and sugar until thick and lemon-colored. Squeeze excess water from the gelatin and melt in 3 tablespoons boiling water. Combine sherry with the gelatin and stir in the

almonds, cherries and chocolate. Fold the egg mixture into the gelatin. Whip the cream and fold into the egg mixture. Pour into a glass bowl and sprinkle with more nuts, chocolate and berries.

Semolina pudding

Heavenly dessert

Caramel pudding
6-8 servings

2 dl (³/₄ cup) sugar
6 dl (2 ½ cups) milk or evaporated milk
3 dl (1 ¼ cups) whipping cream
3 tablespoons sugar
8 eggs
1 ½ teaspoons vanilla extract

Pour the sugar into a 1½-liter (6 cup) loaf pan and place it on the burner over medium heat. Heat until the sugar has melted and turned a warm golden brown. Pour it into the pan, moving the pan to coat the bottom evenly with the caramel. Heat the milk, cream and sugar to boiling. Let cool Whisk the eggs, then whisk them into the milk mixture. Stir in the vanilla. Strain the mixture into the glazed loaf pan. Preheat the oven to 125°C (250°F). Let the pan rest for around 10 minutes before cooking, so that any air bubbles in the mixture can deflate.

Place in a water bath and bake for 2-3 hours. Toward the end of the cooking time, check with the back of a wet spoon, to see if the surface has set, which means that the pudding is cooked. Let cool in the pan, then refrigerate overnight. Unmold onto a platter before serving.

Basic recipe for ice cream
This dessert contains raw eggs Use only safely-checked eggs

4-6 servings

4 egg yolks
2 eggs
100 g (⁷/₈ cup) confectioner's sugar
5 dl (2 cups) whipping cream

Suggestions for flavoring:
2 dl (⁷/₈ cup) jam or berries

Beat egg yolks, eggs and sugar until light and lemon-colored. Whip the cream. Fold the cream into the egg mixture. Fold in the desired flavoring. Pour into a mold and freeze, stirring occasionally when the ice crystals begin to form, or freeze in an ice cream machine.

Pralines-chevre ice cream
with puff pastry
4-6 servings

200 g (1 cup) sugar
1 dl (scant ½ cup) water
100 g (3 ½ oz) *Snøfrisk* (fresh chevre)
1 ½ dl (⅔ cup) whipping cream
2-3 tablespoons almond praline
5 eggs
2 sheets (US: ½ package) frozen puff pastry

Melt half the sugar in a saucepan until golden. Add water and cook to a syrup. Melt the cheese in the syrup and add 1 dl (⅜ cup) of the cream. Let cool slightly and stir in the praline. Beat the eggs and the remaining sugar until light and lemon-colored. Whip the cream. Fold the cheese mixture into the egg mixture, then fold in the cream. Pour into a mold and freeze, stirring occasionally when ice crystals begin to form, or freeze in an ice cream machine. The ice cream should be frozen for at least 6 hours. Defrost the puff pas-

try and cut large circles with a cookie cutter. Bake according to package directions. Let cool. To serve, place a pastry circle in a bowl. Top with ice cream, then arrange berries and a good fruit sauce all around.

Dessert sauces

Fruit sauce
4-6 servings

4 dl (1 2/3 cups) water
4 dl (1 2/3 cups) berry juice concentrate
2 ½ tablespoons potato starch

Combine all ingredients in a saucepan and heat to boiling. Whisk until shiny.

Strawberry sauce
4-6 servings

200 g (½ basket) strawberries
2 ½ dl (1 cup) water
100 g (½ cup) sugar

Clean the berries. Place in a blender with water and sugar and puree until smooth. Heat to boiling, then strain.

Chocolate sauce
4-6 servings

175 g (6 oz) semi-sweet chocolate
1 tablespoon strong coffee
1 tablespoon cognac
2 ½ dl (1 cup) whipping cream

Break the chocolate into bits and place in a saucepan with the remaining ingredients. Heat to boiling. Remove from the heat and stir until smooth.

Vanilla cream
4 servings

2 gelatin sheets
4 egg yolks
2 tablespoons sugar
1 ½ dl (⅔ cup) milk
2 ½ dl (1 cup) whipping cream
2 teaspoons vanilla extract

Soak the gelatin in cold water for 5 minutes to soften. Beat egg yolks and sugar until light and lemon-colored. Combine milk, cream, and egg mixture and heat carefully until the mixture thickens slightly. Squeeze excess water from the gelatin and melt in 3 tablespoons boiling water. Stir into the egg yolk mixture and let cool. Stir in the vanilla. Refrigerate until serving.

Vanilla sauce
4 servings

5 dl (2 cups) milk
2 eggs
2 tablespoons sugar
1 teaspoon cornstarch
2 teaspoons vanilla extract

Heat the milk to boiling. Whisk the eggs with the sugar and cornstarch. Whisk in the hot milk. Pour back into the pan and whisk until thickened. Stir in the vanilla. Let cool completely before serving.

Baked goods

Cream puffs *with lingonberry cream*
12-16 puffs

125 g (4 oz) butter
2 ½ dl (1 cup) water
125 g (⅞ cup) flour
4 eggs

Lingonberry cream
6 dl (2 ½ cups) whipping cream
2-3 dl (1 cup) lingonberry compote

Preheat the oven to 200°C (400°F). Cut the butter into cubes and place in a saucepan with the water. Heat to boiling. Add the flour and stir vigorously until the dough forms a ball. Remove from the heat when the dough leaves the sides of the pan. Let cool slightly. Beat in one egg at a time. It is important to beat well after each egg. The batter should be thick enough to retain its shape. Line an oven sheet with baking parchment. Form mounds of batter with a tablespoon and place on the paper. Bake for 20-25 minutes. Do not open the oven door or the puffs will deflate. Transfer to a rack and let cool. Whip the cream and fold in the berries. Halve the puffs and fill with the cream just before serving. These puffs are also good plain with confectioner's sugar, and of course, you can substitute any other berries for lingonberries.

Carrot cake
4 eggs
2 ½ dl (1 cup) sugar
½ teaspoon vanilla extract
3 ½ dl (1 ½ cups) flour
1 tablespoon cinnamon
2 teaspoons baking soda
½ teaspoon salt
1 dl (scant ½ cup) melted butter
4 dl (1 ⅔ cups) finely grated carrots

Cream cheese frosting
135 g (4 oz) cream cheese
125 g (7/8 cup) confectioner's sugar
1 teaspoon vanilla extract

Carrot cake

Preheat the oven to 180°C (350°F). Beat the egg, sugar and vanilla until thick and lemon-colored. Combine flour, cinnamon, baking powder and salt and add alternately with the butter. Fold in the carrots. Pour into a greased 23 cm (9") round pan. Bake for around 1 hour. Cool completely.

Beat all ingredients in the frosting until smooth and spread over the cake. Garnish with grated carrot, if desired. This cake can be frozen but without frosting.

When completely cold, whip the cream and fold into the egg mixture. Pour into the tart shell and garnish with fruit and berries.

Sponge cake base

30 g (2 ½ tablespoons) sugar and 30 g (3 ½ tablespoons) flour per egg
1 teaspoon baking powder

4 eggs is the norm for a one-layer sponge cake base. They should be at room temperature. Preheat the oven to 160°C (320°F). Beat eggs and sugar until thick and lemon-colored. Sift flour and baking powder together and fold into the egg mixture. Pour into a greased 23 cm (9") springform pan and bake for 30-40 minutes. Cool slightly, then remove from the pan. Cool completely on a rack.

Bavarian cream

This recipe contains uncooked eggs. Use only safety-checked eggs.

6 gelatin sheets
3 eggs
1 dl (scant ½ cup) sugar
3 dl (1 ¼ cups) whipping cream

Flavors

– 3 ½ tablespoons lime juice + 1 pot lemon ver-
  bena, chopped
– 1 ½ dl (2/3 cup) raisins soaked in 1 dl (scant ½
  cup) rum + seeds from a split vanilla bean
– 250 g (9 oz) berries, such as strawberries, rasp-
  berries, lingonberries, black currants or black-
  berries

Soften the gelatin in cold water for 5 minutes. Beat eggs and sugar until light and lemon-col-ored. Squeeze excess water from gelatin and melt

Tart *with pastry cream, fruit and berries*

Pastry

3 ½ dl (1 ½ cups) flour
1 dl (scant ½ cup) confectioner's sugar
125 g (4 oz) butter, in pats
1 egg

Pastry cream

1 vanilla bean or 1 teaspoon vanilla
4 dl (²/₃ cups) milk
6 egg yolks
½ dl (¼ cup) sugar
1 tablespoon cornstarch
1-2 dl (1 cup) whipping cream
fruit and berries

Place pastry ingredients in a food processor and process until the dough forms a ball. Remove from the processor, pack in plastic wrap and refri-gerate for 30 minutes. Preheat the oven to 200°C (400°F). Press the dough into a 22 cm (9") springform pan. Prick with a fork and bake for around 10 minutes. Let cool.

For the pastry cream, split the vanilla bean and scrape out the seeds. Place in a saucepan with the milk, egg yolks, sugar and cornstarch. Heat, stirring constantly, until thickened. Do not allow to boil. Cool quickly by immersing the pan in a larger pan of cold water, stirring occasionally.

in 3 ½ tablespoons boiling water, stirring until completely dissolved. Combine gelatin with one of the flavors and stir into the egg yolk mixture. Whip the cream and fold into the egg yolk mixture. Pour into a large bowl or into individual bowls and refrigerate until stiff.

Marzipan cake

6 eggs
2 dl (⅞ cup) sugar
3 dl (1 ¼ cups) flour
1 teaspoon baking powder
orange juice
1 basket strawberries, chopped
1 recipe Bavarian cream flavored with lime
3 dl (1 ¼ cups) whipping cream
500 g (1 lb) marzipan

Preheat the oven to 160°C (320°F). Beat eggs and sugar until light and lemon-colored. Sift flour and baking powder together and fold into the egg mixture. Pour into a greased 26 cm (10") springform pan. Bake for 45 minutes. Remove from the pan and let cool on a rack. Divide into three layers horizontally and moisten with juice. Place one layer on a serving plate. Spread with Bavarian cream and chopped strawberries. Repeat, then top with remaining layer. Roll out the marzipan and drape over the cake. Cut off excess marzipan at bottom.

Helpful hint
Before decorating the cake, place some parchment paper under the sponge base to keep the plate clean.

Success torte

Nut base
150 g (1 cup) confectioner's sugar
150 g (1 ¹/₃ cups) ground almonds or hazelnuts
4 egg whites

Cream filling
4 egg yolks
1 dl (scant ¹/₂ cup) whipping cream
125 g (²/₃ cup) sugar
1 teaspoon vanilla extract
150 g (5 oz) butter, in pats
60 g semisweet chocolate (optional)

Combine confectioner's sugar and nuts. Stiffly beat the egg whites and fold into the nut mixture. Pour into a 24 cm (9") springform pan. Bake for 30-35 minutes at 160°C. Let cool. Whisk together egg yolks, cream, sugar and vanilla in a large saucepan. Heat, whisking constantly, until thickened. Remove from the heat and stir in the butter in pats. Whisk until creamy and even-textured. Refrigerate (or freeze for a while after it is cooled completely). Place the cake on a serving platter. Spread with pastry cream, forming into mounds, Garnish with chocolate slivers, if desired.

Melt the chocolate and spread onto plastic sheeting. Freeze. Break into bits and use to decorate the cake.

Almond ring cake
18 rings

500 g (5 cups) finely ground almonds
500 g (3 ¹/₂ cups) confectioner's sugar
4 egg whites

Icing
¹/₂ egg white
75 g (¹/₂ cup) confectioner's sugar
¹/₂ teaspoon lemon juice

Combine the almonds and the sugar. Add egg whites to form a stiff dough. Pack in plastic wrap and let rest overnight. Preheat the oven to 200°C (400°F). Roll into finger-thick lengths, or use a cookie press with a wide round tip. Arrange in greased cake rings (can be purchased in specialty stores), making sure that the ends, where joined, are as seamless as possible. Place the rings on oven sheets and bake for around 10 minutes. Cool completely before tapping out of rings. Make a small cone of paper and cut off the tip. Combine ingredients in the icing and spoon into the cone. Pipe zigzags of frosting onto each ring and stack immediately. Almond cake rings freeze well.

Light chocolate cake

Bake for 30-40 minutes. When completely cool, spread with a light chocolate frosting.

Chocolate fondant

Serve this dessert cake warm so that it's still soft and moist inside. It's wonderful when drizzled with espresso syrup and served with ice cream.

300 g (10 oz) semisweet chocolate
250 g (9 oz) butter
2 dl (⁷⁄₈ cup) sugar
5 eggs
3 dl (1 ½ cups) flour
1 teaspoon baking powder
1 teaspoon vanilla extract

Preheat the oven to 180°C (350°F). Melt chocolate and butter together in a large saucepan. Stir in the sugar and let cool slightly. Whisk in one egg at a time, then fold in the dry ingredients. Pour into greased individual molds or into a 23 cm (9") springform pan. Bake for 30-35 minutes. Do not overbake or the cake will dry out. Serve immediately for a runny center. If the cakes are allowed to cool completely, they will set.

Espresso syrup

2 dl (1 cup) strong coffee
½ dl (¼ cup) sugar

Combine coffee and sugar in a small saucepan and reduce over high heat until thick and syrupy. Add more sugar, if needed. Pour half of the syrup over the cakes as soon as they are removed from the oven but are in their pans. Wait until the syrup is absorbed, then drizzle over the rest.

Light chocolate cake

7 dl (3 cups) sugar
300 g (10 oz) soft butter
5 dl (2 cups) milk
4 eggs
8 dl (3 ⅓ cups) flour
2 teaspoons vanilla extract
4 teaspoons baking powder
2½ tablespoons cocoa

Preheat the oven to 180°C (350°F). Place all ingredients into a bowl and mix with an electric mixer until smooth. Pour into a greased oven tray.

Kvæfjord cake

150 g (5 oz) butter
125 g (²/₃ cup) sugar
5 egg yolks
150 g (1 cup) flour
1 teaspoon baking powder
5 tablespoons (¹/₃ cup) milk

Meringue

5 egg whites
180 g (scant 1 cup) sugar
100 g (1 cup) chopped almonds

Filling

2 dl (³/₄ cup) whipping cream
1 teaspoon vanilla extract
5 dl (2 cups) vanilla pastry cream (purchased or homemade)

Preheat the oven to 175°C (350°F). Beat butter and sugar until light and fluffy. Add one egg yolk at a time, beating well after each. Combine flour and baking powder and add alternately with the milk, beating until smooth. Pour into an oven tray lined with baking parchment. Beat the egg whites until almost stiff. Gradually add the sugar, beating until very stiff. Spread the meringue over the cake batter and sprinkle with almonds. Bake for around 25 minutes. Cool and halve the cake. Place one half on a serving platter, meringue side up. Whip the cream and vanilla and fold into the pastry cream. Spread over the cake base. Top with the other cake, meringue side up.

Christmas cookies

Serina cakes

150 g (5 oz) butter
250 g (1 ¾ cups) flour
2 teaspoons baking powder
100 g (½ cup) sugar
1 egg
1 teaspoon vanilla extract
egg white
pearl sugar or crushed sugar cubes

Preheat the oven to 200°C (400°F). Blend the butter, flour and baking powder with a pastry blender until crumbly. Add the sugar, egg and vanilla. Mix lightly but thoroughly. Roll into a long sausage. Cut into small pieces. Roll each piece into a ball and place on baking parchment or on a greased baking sheet. Press the balls down with a fork, brush with egg white and sprinkle with pearl sugar. Bake for around 10 minutes. Cool on a rack and store in an airtight tin.

Berlin wreaths

2 egg yolks, hardcooked
2 egg yolks, raw
125 g (⅝ cup) sugar
250 g (1 cup) butter, softened
300 g (2 cups) flour
1 egg white
pearl sugar or crushed sugar cubes

Mash cooked and raw egg yolks together. Add sugar and beat until light and fluffy. Add butter and flour alternately. Refrigerate for around 1 hour. Preheat the oven to 180°C (350°F). Roll the dough into 10 cm (4") long thin sausages. Form into wreaths, crossing the ends. Place on baking parchment or onto a greased baking sheet. Brush with egg white and sprinkle with pearl sugar. Bake for around 10 minutes. Cool on a rack and store airtight.

Sand cakes

200 g (7 oz) butter
100 g (½ cup) sugar
250 g (1 ¾ cups) flour
100 g (1 cup) ground almonds
1 egg

Beat butter and sugar until light and fluffy. Add the remaining ingredients, mixing well. Refrigerate for 1 hour. Preheat the oven to 175°C (350°F). Grease "sandkake" (small fluted tartlet) tins. Press the dough into the tins. The dough should be very thin. Place on a baking sheet and bake for 10-15 minutes. Let cool slightly before removing from the tins. Cool on a rack. Store airtight or freeze.

White cookie *people*

100 g (3 ½ oz) butter, melted and cooled
3 dl (1 ¼ cups) sugar
2 dl (⅞ cup) milk
1 teaspoon hornsalt (ammonium carbonate) or 1 tablespoon baking powder
1 liter (4 cups) flour

Combine butter, sugar, milk, hornsalt and half the flour, mixing well. Mix in the remaining flour to a stiff dough. Cover with plastic and refrigerate overnight. Preheat the oven to 175°C (350°F). Roll out the dough to a ⅜" thick sheet. Cut figures and place on a greased baking sheet. Bake for around 7 minutes. They should not turn color. Cool completely before decorating with colored frosting.

Goro

¾ dl (⅓ cup) whipping cream
1 egg
1 teaspoon vanilla
125 g (⅔ cup) sugar
500 g (1 lb) flour
1 teaspoon cardamom
325 g (11 oz) butter

Whip the cream. Beat the egg and sugar until thick and lemon-colored. Stir in the cream and vanilla. Set aside a small amount of the flour for rolling out, and combine the dry ingredients. Cut in the butter and stir in the egg mixture, mixing until smooth. Cover and refrigerate for at least 2 hours. Roll out a small amount of the dough at a time and cut pieces with a pastry wheel to fit a goro iron. Bake until crisp and golden. Cool on a rack and store airtight or freeze.

Cones

4 eggs
250 g (1 ¼ cups) sugar
250 g (8 oz) butter, melted
250 g (1 ¾ cups) flour
1 teaspoon cardamom

Beat eggs and sugar until thick and lemon-colored. Stir in the remaining ingredients, mixing well. Grease the "krumkake" iron for the first cookie only. Bake until golden over low heat. Form into a cone while still warm. Cool on a rack and store airtight or freeze.

Helpful hint
Place the warm cookies over an upturned cup to make baskets to fill with berries and whipped cream.

Back from left: Prune twist, lingonberry cake and apple twist. Front from left: Marzipan bread, coconut horns and filled sweet buns.

Basic sweet yeast dough
(large portion)

You can make six different sweet breads with this dough

1 liter (quart) milk
100 g (3 ½ oz) fresh yeast
2 eggs
3 dl (1 ¼ cups) sugar
2 teaspoons baking powder
4 teaspoons cardamom
300 g (10 oz) butter
3 liters (12 ½ cups) flour

Heat the milk to lukewarm. Crumble the yeast into the milk and stir in the eggs. Combine sugar, baking powder and cardamom in a large bowl. Cut the butter into cubes and knead into the sugar mixture. Add the milk and gradually knead in the flour with a dough hook until it forms a ball. Cover and let rise until doubled.

Apple kuchen – *variation 1*

$^1/_6$ of the basic dough, risen once

Filling
2 $^1/_2$ dl (1 cup) vanilla pastry cream (purchased or homemade)
3 apples
1 dl (scant $^1/_2$ cup) sliced almonds

Grease a 20x25 cm (8x10") pan. Roll the dough into a rectangle large enough to fit and place in the pan. Spread with vanilla cream. Cut the apples into wedges and arrange over the cream. Sprinkle with almonds. Cover and let rise for around 20 minutes. Preheat the oven to 200°C (400°F). Bake for around 35 minutes. Cool on a rack. Serve lukewarm, with a drizzle of powdered sugar glaze and whipped cream alongside.

Prune kuchen – *variation 2*

$^1/_6$ of the basic dough, risen once

Filling
2 $^1/_2$ dl (1 cup) vanilla pastry cream (purchased or homemade)
150 g (5 oz) pitted prunes
75 g (2 $^1/_2$ oz) walnut halves

Grease a 20x25 cm (8x10") pan. Roll the dough into a rectangle large enough to fit and place in the pan. Spread with vanilla cream and arrange prunes and walnuts over the cream. Cover and let rise for around 20 minutes. Preheat the oven to 200°C (400°F). Bake for around 35 minutes. Cool on a rack. Serve lukewarm, with whipped cream alongside.

Coconut horns – *variation 3*

12 horns

$^1/_6$ of the basic dough, risen once

Filling
125 g (4 oz) cream cheese
1 dl (scant $^1/_2$ cup) coconut
1 dl (scant $^1/_2$ cup) sugar
2 teaspoons cinnamon
1 dl (scant $^1/_2$ cup) raisins (optional)
chopped mint
beaten egg

Divide the dough in two and roll each into a circle. Cut each circle into three triangles. Combine all ingredients in the filling and spread over the triangles. Roll up. Place on baking parchment, cover and let rise for around 20 minutes. Preheat the oven to 225°C (425°F). Brush with egg. Bake for around 15 minutes. Cool on a rack.

Lingonberry cake – *variation 4*

$^1/_6$ of the basic dough, risen once

Filling
2 $^1/_2$ dl (1 cup) vanilla pastry cream (purchased or homemade
2 $^1/_2$ dl (1 cup) lingonberries
2 tablespoons sugar
beaten egg

Roll out the dough to a 30x35 cm (12x14") rectangle. Spread with vanilla cream and sprinkle with berries and sugar. Roll up from the long side. Cut into 12 pieces and arrange in a greased 23 cm (9") springform pan. Cover and let rise for around 30 minutes. Preheat the oven to 200°C (400°F). Brush with egg and bake for around 30 minutes. Let cool on a rack. Serve lukewarm, preferably with a drizzle of confectioner is sugar glaze.

Marzipan length – *variation 5*

⅙ of the basic dough, risen once

Filling
4 tablespoons (1/4 cup) vanilla pastry cream (purchased or homemade)
250 g (8 oz) marzipan
1 dl (scant ½ cup) shelled pistachio nuts

Beaten egg
confectioner's sugar glaze
coarsely chopped pistachio nuts

Roll the dough into a 30x35 cm (12-14") rectangle. Spread the vanilla cream in a strip down the middle and cover with thin slices of marzipan. Sprinkle with nuts. Make 10 diagonal cuts in the dough from each side toward the middle (toward the filling) and drape the dough strands over the filling alternately from each side to enclose it completely. Cover and let rise for 30 minutes. Preheat the oven to 200°C (400°F). Brush with egg and bake for around 20 minutes. Let cool on a rack and serve lukewarm with confectioner's sugar glaze and top with nuts.

Filled rolls – *variation 6*
12 rolls

⅙ of the basic dough, risen once

Filling
Candy covered chocolate or chocolate chips
Beaten egg
Confectioner's sugar glaze

Divide the dough into 12 pieces of equal size and form round balls. Make a hole in each and fill with 6 candies or chocolate chips. Close the hole and place the rolls on a greased oven tray, hole down. Cover and let rise for 30 minutes. Preheat the oven to 225°C (245°F). Bake for around 13 minutes. Cool on a rack. Serve lukewarm with confectioner's sugar glaze. Garnish with more chocolate, if desired. These are even good without filling.

Coconut cream rolls
12-14 rolls

3 ½ dl (1 ½ cups) milk
50 g (1 ¾ oz) fresh yeast
100 g (3 ½ oz) butter
1 dl (scant ½ cup) sugar
½ teaspoon cardamom
1 liter (4 cups) flour
1 portion egg cream, see page 258
confectioner's sugar, coconut

Heat the milk to 37°C (98°F). Dissolve the yeast in the milk. Melt the butter, cool slightly and add, along with the sugar and cardamom. Sift in the flour and knead into a soft dough. Cover and let rise until almost doubled. Roll smooth balls and press them down in the center. Place on an oven sheet and let rise until doubled. Preheat the oven to 250°C (450°F). Place a generous spoonful of egg cream in the center of each roll. Bake for 10-12 minutes. Let cool on a rack. Spread confectioner's sugar glaze on each roll and dip into a plate of coconut.

Coconut cream rolls

Christmas bread

2 loaves

125 g (4 oz) butter
5 dl (2 cups) milk
50 g (1 ¾ oz) fresh yeast
125 g (⅝ cup) sugar
650 g (4 ⅓ cups) flour
1 teaspoon cardamom
150 g (5 oz) raisins
citron (optional)
beaten egg

Melt the butter and add the milk. Dissolve the yeast in the milk mixture. Stir in the sugar. Knead in the flour and cardamom, kneading until the dough is smooth and elastic. Cover and let rise until doubled, around 40 minutes. Turn out onto a floured board and divide in two. Divide the raisins (and citron) evenly between the two and knead into two large round balls. Using a sharp knife, cut a line around the edge of the balls and press them down in the center, to prevent them from cracking so easily. The dough can also be placed in greased 2-liter (quart) loaf pans. Cover and let rise for 30-40 minutes. Preheat the oven to 175°C (350°F). Bake on the lowest shelf for 20-40 minutes. Let cool on a rack.

Astrid's wreath, sweet roll, princess cake and cinnamon rolls

100 g (3 ½ oz) butter
3 ½ dl (1 ½ cups) milk
50 g (1 ¾ oz) fresh yeast
1 egg
100 g (1/2 cup) sugar
1 teaspoon cardamom
½ teaspoon baking powder
600 g (4 cups) flour

Melt the butter and add the milk. Dissolve the yeast in the milk mixture and stir in the egg. Sift together the dry ingredients and add. Knead until smooth and elastic. Cover and let rise until doubled, at least 45 minutes. Form the dough into the desired shape.

Astrid's wreath

Filling

200 g (2 cups) ground almonds
150 g (1 cup) confectioner's sugar
1 egg white
1–2 tablespoons water

Topping

Vanilla or rum cream

Roll the dough into a 75x20 cm (30x8") length. Combine almonds, confectioner's sugar, egg white and water. Spoon the almond mixture along one long end. Roll together. Form into a "wreath" on a baking sheet. Cover and let rise for 20 minutes. Preheat the oven to 225°C (425°F). It's a good idea to place custard cups in the two "holes" during baking so that the pretzel doesn't spread out and run together. Brush with

beaten egg, sprinkle with pearl sugar or sliced almonds and bake for around 20 minutes.

Sweet roll

Filling
Vanilla or rum cream

Topping
currants
sugar
cinnamon

Form the dough into two lengths and place them on an oven sheet. Make a groove down the center of each and fill with pastry cream. Sprinkle with currants, cinnamon and sugar. Cover and let rise for 20 minutes. Preheat the oven to 225°C (425°F). Brush with egg and bake for 15-20 minutes.

Princess cake and cinnamon rolls

Filling
100 g (3 ½ oz) butter, softened
2 teaspoons cinnamon
3 tablespoons sugar
vanilla cream
raisins

Divide the sheet into thirds. Roll one into a circle and place in the bottom and up the sides of a 24-26 cm (10") spring form pan. Roll the other two pieces into 60x30 cm (24x12") rectangles. Spread each length butter and sprinkle with a mixture of cinnamon and sugar. Spread with a little vanilla cream, sprinkle with raisins and roll up lengthwise. Cut the rolls into 3-4 cm (1 ½") slices. Place some rolls, cut side down, in the dough-lined pan. Top with vanilla cream. Place the remaining rolls on an oven sheet. Cover and let rise for 20 minutes. Preheat the oven to 225°C (245°F). Brush with egg and bake the cinnamon rolls for 12-15 minutes and the cake for 40 minutes.

Smaller baked goods

Basic dough
You can make six different breads with this dough

100 g (3 ½ oz) butter
1 liter (4 cups) water
100 g (3 ½ oz) fresh yeast
2 teaspoons salt
around 3 liter (12 ½ cups) all-purpose flour

Melt the butter and add the water. Dissolve the yeast in the lukewarm liquid. Add salt and stir until the dough sticks together and leaves the sides of the bowl. Cover with plastic wrap and let rise until doubled, at least 30 minutes. Divide into six pieces of equal size and make the following variations:

Herb bread – *variation 1*
1 bread

⅙ of basic dough, risen once

Filling
1 ½ dl (⅔ cup) finely chopped spinach leaves
125 g (4 oz) garlic cream cheese
beaten egg
grated Jarlsberg cheese

Preheat the oven to 200°C (400°F). Roll the dough into a 25x35 cm (10x14") rectangle. Spread with cream cheese and sprinkle with spinach. Roll up from the long side. Place seam side down on a baking sheet lined with parchment paper. Cut diagonal slits in the roll with a sharp knife. Cover with plastic and let rise until doubled. Brush with egg, sprinkle with cheese and bake for around 35 minutes.

Cheese spirals with ham
– *variation 2*
9-10 spirals

⅙ of basic dough, risen once

Filling
9 thin turkey ham slices
2 dl (1 cup) grated Jarlsberg cheese
1 dl (½ cup) finely chopped chives
beaten egg
grated Jarlsberg cheese

Preheat the oven to 225°C (425°F). Roll the dough into a 20x30 (8x12") rectangle. Top with ham and sprinkle with cheese and chives. Roll up from the long side. Cut into 9-10 slices with a sharp knife. Place on a baking sheet lined with parchment paper. Cover and let rise until doubled. Brush with egg and sprinkle with cheese. Bake for around 12 minutes and let cool on a rack.

Peanut knots – *variation 3*
9-10 knots

⅙ of basic dough, risen once
1 ½ dl (⅔ cup) coarsely chopped salted peanuts
beaten egg
coarsely chopped salted peanuts

Preheat the oven to 225°C (425° F). Knead the peanuts into the dough. Divide into 9-10 pieces of equal size. Roll each piece into a finger-thick sausage around 12 cm (5") long. Form into a knot and place on a baking sheet lined with parchment paper. Cover and let rise for around 15 minutes. Brush with egg and sprinkle with peanuts. Bake for around 10 minutes and let cool on a rack.

Back from left: Large crescents, herb bread and basil crescents. Front from left: Peanut knots, cheese twists with ham and carrot rolls.

Large horns – *variation 4*
4 horns

⅙ of basic dough, risen once
100 g (3 ½ oz) fresh chevre or cream cheese
4 tablespoons (¼ cup) chopped sun-dried tomatoes, drained
beaten egg
grated cheese
1 ½ teaspoons caraway seed

Preheat the oven to 200°C (400°F). Roll the dough into a circle, around 35 cm (14") in diameter. Divide into 4 parts and spread with cheese. Spoon 1 tablespoon chopped tomato on each and roll up to make large horns. Place on a baking sheet lined with parchment paper. Cover and let rise for 20 minutes. Brush with egg, sprinkle with cheese and caraway seed. Bake for 15-17 minutes and cool on a rack.

Basil horns – *variation 5*

8 horns

¹/₆ of basic dough, risen once
2 dl (1 cup) grated Jarlsberg cheese
1 dl (¹/₂ cup) shredded fresh basil
beaten egg
1 dl (¹/₂ cup) sunflower seeds

Preheat the oven to 225°C (425°F). Roll the dough into a circle, around 35 cm (14") in diameter. Divide into 8 triangles and sprinkle with cheese and basil. Roll up to make horns. Place on a baking sheet lined with parchment paper. Cover and let rise for 20 minutes. Brush with egg and sprinkle with seeds. Bake for around 12 minutes and let cool on a rack.

Carrot roll cluster – *variation 6*

8 rolls

¹/₆ of basic dough, risen once
2 dl (1 cup) grated carrots
beaten egg
sunflower seeds

Preheat the oven to 200°C (400°F). Knead the carrots into the dough. Divide into 8 pieces of equal size and form into balls. Place one ball in the center of a baking sheet lined with parchment paper. Place the remaining balls in a ring all around. Cover and let rise for 20 minutes. Brush with egg and sprinkle with seeds. Bake for around 15 minutes and let cool on a rack.

Breakfast rolls

30 rolls

2 dl (1 cup) rolled oats
250 g (8 oz) cottage cheese
50 g (1 ³/₄ oz) fresh yeast
5 dl (2 cups) lukewarm water
1 teaspoon salt
13-14 dl (5 ¹/₃ – 5 ³/₄ cups) whole-wheat flour

Combine oats and cottage cheese and let sit overnight. Dissolve the yeast in the water and stir in the oat mixture, salt and most of the flour. Knead well, until the dough leaves the side of the bowl. Cover and let rise for 30 minutes. Punch down the dough. Turn out onto a floured board and knead in the remaining flour. Divide into 30 pieces of equal size and form into round balls. Place the balls on a greased baking sheet, cover and let rise for around 30 minutes. Preheat the oven to 230°C (450°F). Bake for around 20 minutes. Serve slightly warm. These freeze well. Reheat for 5-8 minutes.

Bread

Unless otherwise stated, make all bread according to the following directions:

– All ingredients should be room temperature.
– Liquid (water or milk) should be 35-37° C (94-98° F).
– Dissolve yeast and salt in the liquid.
– Stir after each addition of flour, so that coarse particles can absorb liquid.
– After kneading, let the dough rise until double in size. Punch down, knead again and divide into loaves.
– Final rising can take place in the oven set to 40°C (104°F) with a cup of boiling water in a tray on the oven floor.

- Place the breads into an oven preheated to 230-240°C (450-465°F). Lower the temperature to 180-200°C (350-400°F), and bake for 30-45 minutes.
- Fresh yeast is used in all recipes. If using dry yeast, use one-fourth the amount of yeast.
- Add dry yeast along with the flour.

Basic dough

The basic dough can be used as is, but it also can be used as a basis for variations. The advantage is that you can bake several types at once, because rising and baking times, as well as temperature, are the same for all the breads. This recipe yields around 3 kg (6 ½ lb) basic dough.

1 ¼ liter (5 cups) water
50 g (1 ¾ oz) yeast
25 g (4 teaspoons) salt
300 g (2 cups) whole-wheat flour (finely or coarsely ground)
300 g (2 cups) whole-rye flour (finely or coarsely ground)
around 1 ¼ kg (2 ½ lb) all-purpose flour
2 tablespoons oil

Prepare according to general directions.

Sunflower seed bread
– variation 1

1 kg (2 ¼ lb) basic dough
150 g (5 oz) sunflower seeds

Three-grain bread
– variation 2

1 kg (2 ¼ lb) basic dough
150 g (5 oz) rye kernels
2 ½ dl (1 cup) water
½ teaspoon salt
2 dl (scant 1 cup) flaxseed

Soak the kernels in the water for at least 15 minutes before kneading into the dough. Add extra all-purpose flour if necessary.

Whole-wheat bread
– variation 3
1 kg (2 ¼ lb) basic dough
3 ½ dl (1 ½ cups) wheat kernels
2 ½ dl (1 cup) water
½ teaspoon salt

Soak the kernels in the water for at least 15 minutes before kneading into the dough. Add extra all-purpose flour if necessary.

Walnut bread
– variation 4

1 kg (2 ¼ lb) basic dough
50-75 g (½ cup) chopped walnuts

Canary bread
– variation 5

1 kg (2 ¼ lb) basic dough
200-300 g (7-10 oz) drained and chopped sun-dried tomatoes
4 tablespoons (¼ cup) chopped fresh herbs, such as oregano, rosemary and/or coriander

Fiber bomb
It would be hard to find a coarser bread than this one baked with whole grain flour and bran.

2 loaves

1 liter (4 cups) water
4 teaspoons salt
1 tablespoon 7% vinegar or lemon juice
1 ¾ dl (¾ cup) whole wheat kernels
4 ½ dl (1 ¾ cups) wheat bran
or 2 dl (¾ cup) oat bran + 2 ½ dl (1 cup) wheat bran

1 ¾ dl (¾ cup) finely ground whole-rye flour
3 ½ tablespoons flaxseed
3 ½ tablespoons sunflower seeds, lightly crushed
9 - 11 dl (3 ¾ 4 ⅓ cups) finely ground whole-wheat flour
50 g (1 ¾ oz) fresh yeast

Combine the first 8 ingredients and stir into a thick gruel. Let steep for at least one hour. Add some of the flour and crumble in part of the yeast. Stir until all flour is moistened. Stir in flour until around ¾ of the entire amount has been added. Stir as long as you have the strength, if stirring by hand, 10 minutes if using a machine. Cover with plastic and let rest for 30 minutes. Make a mound of most of the remaining flour on a board. Turn out the dough onto the flour. With floured hands, knead until the dough is smooth and elastic (stretch, fold together, repeating as necessary). Divide the dough into two parts and shape each piece first into a ball and then into a loaf. Place in greased loaf pans. Set the oven thermostat at 40°C (104°F) with the oven tray on the lowest rill and the rack just under the center of the oven. When the oven has reached 40°C (104°F), place the pans on the rack and pour 1 cup boiling water into the oven tray. Close the door immediately. Let the breads rise for 30 minutes. Remove carefully from the oven. Increase the oven temperature to 220°C (425°F) (use the "pizza function" if your oven has one).

When the oven has reached 220°C (425°F), place the pans on the rack and pour another cup of boiling water into the oven tray. Close the door, lower the temperature to 185°C (375°F), and bake for 40-45 minutes. Remove the breads from the pans immediately and cool on a rack.

Sunflower seed bread

made in a bread machine
1 loaf

Place ingredients in the machine in the following order:
2 ½ dl (1 cup) water
1 tablespoon oil (optional)
1 tablespoon dark corn or sugar syrup or molasses
1 ½ teaspoons salt
1 ¾ dl (¾ cup) finely ground whole-wheat flour
4 ¼ dl (1 ¾ cups) all-purpose flour
1 dl (scant ½ cup) sunflower seeds
1 ½ teaspoons dry yeast (always dry yeast in a bread machine)

Bake according to directions for machine. Of course this recipe can be used for baking in a regular oven.

Mediterranean bread

with garlic and olives

2 loaves

Day 1:
5 dl (2 cups) water
3 ½ tablespoons yogurt or sour milk
25 g (1 oz) fresh yeast
2 dl (¾ cup) rye flour
2 dl (1 cup) all-purpose flour
2 teaspoons salt

Make according to general directions. Cover and let rest for 10-15 hours.

Day 2:
Uncover the dough and add
2 ½ dl (1 cup) rye flour
2 tablespoons olive oil
2-4 garlic cloves, minced
as many olives as you like, both green and black, sliced
a little liquid from the olives
around 1 liter (4 cups) all-purpose flour

Stir together and add enough all-purpose flour to make a relatively soft dough. Cover and let rise for 1 hour. Punch down and knead again. Cover and let rise for 1 hour. Form into 2 loaves. For pretty loaves, place the dough in floured baskets. Let rise at room temperature for around 30 minutes, if desired. Preheat the oven to 250°C (475°F). Just before baking, tip the loaves out onto a greased baking sheet. Remove the baskets and bake for 10 minutes. Lower the temperature to 200°C (400°F) and bake for 20 minutes.

English milk bread

7 loaves

1 ⅓ liter (5 1/3 cups) full-fat milk
3 dl (1 ¼ cups) water
2 eggs
2 tablespoons salt
60 g (¼ cup) butter
4 liters (16 ¾ cups) all purpose flour

Nan bread
10 flat breads

500 g (3 ⅓ cups) all-purpose flour
1 tablespoon dry yeast
1 tablespoon sugar
2 ½ dl (1 cup) buttermilk or cultured milk

2 ½ dl (1 cup) full fat milk
3 tablespoons soybean oil

Combine all ingredients and let rise until double.
Divide into 10 pieces of equal size and roll flat.
Bake quickly on a grill, first on the one side, then
on the other.

Index

Other Photographers

Børjesson, Alf / EFF: page: 37, 45, 46, 59.

Eide, Per: page: cover; fjord fish and sea, 104 bottom, 27 top, 30 top, 32, 44 top, 51, 58, 60, 63, 64 top, 67, 69, 116, 127 top, 157.

Løken, Bård / Samfoto, page: cover: lamb.

Søby, Øystein / Samfoto, page: cover: field.

Picture sources:

TINE (Norwegian Dairies): page 7, 14, 15, 17, 21, 122, 131, 141, 142, 144, 151.

Information Office for Meat: page 87, 88, 95, 98, 100.

Information Office for Eggs and White Meat: page 13, 70, 77, 78, 79, 139.

Export Office for Fish: page 34, 37, 45, 48, 49, 59, 62, 66.